Contents

Map of the book		4
Introduction		6
UNIT 1 •	The Telephone Answering Machine	10
UNIT 2 •	'So you wanna keep fit, huh?'	12
UNIT 3 •	Inter-City 125	14
UNIT 4 •	Bibi Khanym and the Origin of the Muslim Veil	16
UNIT 5 •	Who's who?	18
UNIT 6 •	Radio Advertisements	20
UNIT 7 •	Terminal One	22
UNIT 8 •	The Touch of Death	24
UNIT 9 •	Dial-A-Recipe	26
UNIT 10 •	The Weather Forecast	28
UNIT 11 •	Buying a New Car	30
UNIT 12 •	The London Marathon	32
UNIT 13 •	The People's Republic of China: Facts and Figures	34
UNIT 14 •	A Valuable Collection?	36
UNIT 15 •	What's in a Name?	38
UNIT 16 •	'Value for Money'	40
UNIT 17 •	Programming the Video	42
UNIT 18 •	The Department Store	44
UNIT 19 •	Radio Phone-In	46
UNIT 20 •	First Aid	48
Tapescript		50
Answer key		

Map of the book

Unit	Language and listening skills	Vocabulary	Structures
1	Understanding and responding to a telephone answering machine • Specific information 　Discrimination	Personal details, dates, days, times	Tense review, *Wh-* questions, *to be nervous about*, *to have to do*
2	Instructions, advantages and disadvantages • Specific information 　Discrimination 　Detail	Health and exercise, parts of the body, movements, personality	Imperatives, adverbs of manner
3	Public announcements, making inferences • Specific information 　Detail 　Gist	Train travel, places, fast food	Passive, conditional sentences, polite requests
4	Story telling, speculation • Gist 　Discrimination 　Development	Stories and legends, exotic parts of the world	Simple past and past perfect review, narrative links
5	Descriptions, dictation, self-introduction • Specific information 　Further information	Introductions, descriptions, personality	Tense review, prepositions, adjective order
6	Essential information, comparing important and unimportant • Specific information 　Gist 　Distinguishing sounds	Radio ads and consumer programmes, domestic electrical equipment	Tense review
7	Airport announcements • Specific information	Airports and air travel	Present continuous forms, formal and polite requests, *do* to stress importance
8	Narrative, speculation • Gist 　Discrimination 　Specific information 　Development	Short stories, adolescence	Past perfect tense, future conditional (pos. and neg.)
9	Instructions, making notes with key words • Specific information 　Discrimination 　Development	Ingredients, cooking and food	Imperatives, sequence markers (*first, then, next,* etc.)

Unit	Language and listening skills	Vocabulary	Structures

10	The future, predicting
	● Gist
	   Specific information
	   Distinguishing sounds
		The weather, European countries	Future forms with *will*

11	Making comparisons; speculation, probability and prediction, discussion
	● Detail
	   Logic
	   Distinguishing sounds
		Cars, features and components, prices	Comparatives, superlatives, question forms, tags

12	Ambitions, feelings, directions, past narrative ● Specific information	London, running a marathon	Past forms tense review, prepositions
13	Facts and figures, factual presentation ● Gist Specific information	Modern China, inventions, land, population, statistics	Simple present tense review
14	The past, giving reasons ● Gist Specific information	Collecting, badges, logos, trademarks, advertising	Gerund and infinitive (*I began to collect/collecting*)
15	Logic of continuous discourse ● Gist Specific information	Names, their power to influence behaviour in advertising	General tense review
16	Understanding and making comparisons ● Detail	Consumer goods, features and performance	*to get . . . (something) . . . with . . . (something) . . .*
17	Sequence of instructions, clarifying ● Specific information	Operating machinery (eg. video)	*to have to do . . .* , question forms with conditional, (*What would happen if . . .*)
18	Identifying location, prices, likelihood and possibility ● Specific information Informed speculation	Shopping, food, clothes, prices	Imperative, language of speculation (*may be/could be/perhaps*)
19	Advice and suggestions ● Gist Specific information	Personal problems; teenage problems, baldness, smoking	Giving advice (*Why don't you . . ./If I were you I'd . . . Have you ever thought about . . .*)
20	Instructions and advice ● Gist Specific information	First aid, dressing cuts and grazes	Present tense review, simple past conditional review, imperative for instructions

Introduction

When we listen it is because we are interested in gossip, because we need to know how to get to a friend's new apartment, so that we can recognise a stranger we have to meet at the railway station, or in order to follow a recipe or operate a machine. We listen for a reason. We listen with a purpose. We have an objective.

Listening in Action tries to re-create or simulate and then exploit the purposes we have when we listen in our everyday lives. It contains a wide variety of questions, exercises and activities, many of them in the form of tasks to carry out or problems to solve.

Conscious listening is usually accompanied or followed by some kind of action or reaction. We make notes, ask questions, discuss or write a response. So, although **Listening in Action** is primarily a collection of supplementary listening practice material, it also contains discussion questions, writing activities and integrated project ideas. It tries to reflect real-life listening situations as closely as possible.

To the student

Listening in Action contains 20 Units. Each Unit is divided into several sections.

Organisation of the material

Pre-listening discussion questions

There are questions to discuss before you listen to the tape. These are designed to help you to start thinking and talking about the subject of the Unit before you listen to the tape. They should help you to remember useful words and phrases and they should prepare you for the listening passages on the tape.

Intensive and extensive listening

The exercises in each Unit are divided into several Parts. These Parts practise *intensive* and *extensive* listening skills. Intensive listening activities usually need you to listen carefully for a specific piece of information or for a detail. Extensive listening activities usually need you to form a general opinion or to listen for the main ideas in what you listen to.

Language skills

There is a detailed list of the language skills you will practise in each Unit in the Map of the Book on pages 4–5 of this book.

How much do you need to understand?

In order to carry out the activities, do the tasks and solve the problems in this material you will need to understand *some* of the information you listen to. If you can complete the activities successfully it is because you have understood what you needed to know.

New words

There may be a lot of new words you don't recognise in some of the recordings you listen to. Many of these words will not be so important just now. Do you understand every word you hear or read in your first language?

Guessing meanings

You will probably be able to guess the meanings of many new words, and that is a very good way to learn. You are almost certainly wrong if you think you should memorise every new word you hear or read. It's an impossible task anyway!

Additional activities

When you have finished working from the tape there are some additional activities to do. These are important even though most of them don't involve listening directly. They follow up the listening skills you have practised and provide speaking, writing and sometimes reading work to reinforce and consolidate the work you have done from the tape.

General advice

Your teacher is not the only person you know who can speak English. Listen to the other students in your class, too. You can almost certainly learn from them and they can almost certainly learn from you.

Other ways to improve your listening skills include listening to:
- English-speaking radio stations
- English-speaking satellite TV channels
- English-language films (but not those which have been dubbed!)
- other people's conversations
- public announcements (e.g. at railway stations and airports, etc.)
- songs (e.g. on record, audio or video tape).

To the self-study student

If you are using this book on your own, without a teacher, these additional notes are also for you.

How to use this material

For you it is probably a good idea to begin at Unit 1 and work steadily through the Units in chronological order (i.e. the order in which they appear in the book). However, if you are also studying from a course book you can use **Listening in action** to follow up the topics in that coursebook. That will mean using the Units in this material in a different order.

Level

You will probably notice that the first five Units are a little easier than Units 6–10, and that Units 11–15 are a little more difficult. Units 16–20 may not seem much more difficult than Units 11–15, but if they do, don't worry. No two students are ever at exactly the same level, especially at this pre-intermediate stage. Some 'good' students often find 'easy' materials a little more difficult than they expect, while some 'slower' students might find the same material relatively easy.

The Answer Key

Use the Answer Key to check all your answers to any one Unit at the same time, after you have finished working through that Unit.

Control the material – don't let it control you!

Take it easy. Relax. Don't be anxious. No one works well if they're nervous. This material is designed to help you. It is not a test or an exam. You are in control of it. You can stop the tape, re-wind and listen again as often as you want to. But do remember that you can't stop real people and re-wind their conversation (although you can, of course, ask them to repeat what they've just said, a little more slowly or clearly). In a real English-speaking situation you will need to understand the important information in the language you listen to as you hear it. As you work through this book try to rely less and less on the PAUSE and RE-WIND buttons on your cassette player, and follow the instructions for each activity very carefully.

Tapescripts

DO NOT READ THE TAPESCRIPTS BEFORE YOU WORK THROUGH THE UNITS! The tapescripts are there to help you with new words and expressions *after* you have worked through the exercises and activities. You should only refer to them before you have finished a Unit if you simply cannot understand what you are listening to.

Pre-listening discussion questions and additional activities

The pre-listening discussion questions at the beginning and the additional activities at the end of each Unit are primarily designed for students working with a teacher in a class. However, you should read through and think about the pre-listening discussion questions before you listen to the tape.

Additional activities

Many of the additional activities are possible for self-study students but you will not normally be able to check your work.

To the teacher

You should read the introductory notes to students, above, before reading these notes for teachers.

Pre-intermediate students

Listening in Action is a collection of supplementary listening skills material for pre-intermediate students.

Structures and vocabulary

Such students will, generally, be familiar with the principal tense forms of English and the constructions through which they can be realised. They will also, generally, require repeated, continuous and extended practice at selecting and using these forms appropriately and correctly. Such students, typically, have a basic 'general purposes' vocabulary. They are approaching the stage in their language learning careers where they require both substantial consolidation and functional extension. Their passive competence will be considerably greater than their active competence.

Attitudes

They may well be about to develop negative attitudes to continued study because of failure to grasp all the new language they have had to face since being 'beginners', frustration at not having fulfilled their (often unrealistic) and their teachers' expectations, or boredom with the seemingly endless repetition and drilling which is often a characteristic feature of classroom teaching to elementary students. Students at a pre-intermediate level often require an overall morale and motivation booster. They often get no further than pre-intermediate level, and this is rarely anything to do with the intrinsic difficulty of the language they are trying to learn.

The material – topic-oriented

Listening in Action is essentially topic-oriented. One of its principal objectives is to present twenty *interesting* units.

Task-based

It is task-based in that most of the tape-exploitation material requires students to identify more or less detailed (intensive-extensive) information markers in order to be able to answer questions or complete exercises and activities.

Authenticity

Some of the recorded material was not originally produced for language-learning purposes. In that sense it is *authentic*. The rest has been devised to resemble 'real-world' material as closely as possible, the aim being to attempt to re-create in the classroom many of the essential features of the situations in which students will need to listen to and understand language outside the classroom. In that sense much of the material is 'authentic-seeming'.

Grading and level

Listening in Action is not structurally graded. However, the Map of the Book (pp 4–5) describes the main linguistic objectives for each Unit and sets these out in relation to topics, vocabulary, listening skills and language structures.
In very general terms, most students will find Units 1–5 easier than the remaining Units. These are intended as broadly introductory Units.
Units 6–19 introduce material which is gradually more linguistically complex presented in tasks which are increasingly cognitively more demanding. Unit 20 is a consolidation and review Unit and as such will probably be found to be rather easier than the Units immediately preceding it.

Order of use

It is important that you use the Units in this material in the order in which you consider them to be most appropriate for *your* students. Some students will find it easier to cope with a long piece of listening on a familiar theme than with a short piece on something quite new. Accents, speaking speed, task types, cultural distance are just some of the factors which affect students' perception of a lesson as 'easy' or 'difficult', challenging or trivial, stimulating or boring. The Map of the Book is designed to help you select material which is appropriate for a given class at a given time.

Ways of using Listening in Action	There are basically two ways of using material like **Listening in Action**: the 'daily dose' approach and the 'thematic link'.
The 'daily dose'	With the 'daily dose' approach the teacher includes a specific listening skill development activity as part of every lesson. If your lessons are of two or more hours you can use the 'daily dose' approach with this material without distorting the skills balance of your lesson planning. If you see your class for only one hour per day, or, worse, for no more than one hour per week, you will have to decide which of the language skills to concentrate on in each lesson since a 40–50 minute lesson which evenly practises all four skills in any depth requires meticulous planning and timing which cannot allow for the natural deviation from all planning which is a characteristic of lively, successful classrooms.
The 'thematic link'	The 'thematic link' approach is where the teacher looks for a piece of listening material which will support the topic or theme of work currently being done in the students' main coursebook. This material can be used with such an approach and you should not be reluctant to select only a few activities from an appropriate Unit, and return to the others later in the course if necessary.
Approaching a Unit	**Listening in Action** contains sufficient material (basic + additional activities) for a total of between roughly 30–55 classroom hours. If you have the luxury of one two-hour 'listening lesson' per week or are teaching intensively, say, five six-hour days per week, you can use the material *extensively*, giving plenty of time to the pre-listening discussion questions and the additional activities.
Pre-listening discussion questions	The pre-listening discussion questions are intended to help to activate students' passive vocabulary by encouraging the contribution of ideas and opinions closely related to those which form the substance of the taped material. They should help students to move into the listening stage with a receptive and 'informed' mental set.
Questions, exercises and activities	The questions, exercises and activities which form the main body of each Unit are clearly labelled according to the skills being practised and clearly set out the procedure students should follow (e.g. Listen *then* answer; Answer *while* listening, etc).
Number of listenings	The number of listenings required is specified throughout the book but you should not hesitate to increase the number of listenings if your students ask for or appear to need it. This is *support* material, not a test.
Additional activities	The additional activities are useful in 'rounding off' a Unit's work, often at the same time as extending it, and they also provide some of the less conventional classroom work which students often find so motivating so long as their teacher is firmly behind it.
Preparation	**Listening in Action** will be more enjoyable to work with if you ALWAYS read through each Unit, the Answer Key and Tapescript before you teach from it. Listen to the tape, make notes of any important points from it you want to include in your lesson and write down the tape counter numbers for the start of each section of the tape. Try to anticipate the difficulties your students may have with a Unit and prepare material, examples and explanations beforehand. Finally, be prepared to explain to students who may believe that they should try to memorise every new word they hear on the tape that not only will that not help them, but that it will actually hinder their progress.
	I hope that you have as much pleasure teaching from **Listening in Action** as I had compiling the material and devising the exercises.

UNIT 1 The Telephone Answering Machine

Are you nervous about speaking English on the telephone? Do you hate telephone answering machines?

Pre-listening discussion questions

1) Why are some people nervous about using the telephone? Are you? If so, why?
2) What are the advantages and disadvantages of telephone answering machines? Write two lists.
3) Have you ever used one? What happened?

PART A

Listening for specific information

Read questions 1 and 2 and then listen to Part A of the tape. Answer while you are listening.

1) What's the name of the school?

a) The Oxford School of English ☐   c) The Oxbridge School of English ☐

b) The Cambridge School of English ☐

2) What's the school's telephone number? _____

Now read questions 3 and 4 and then listen to Part A of the tape again. Answer while you are listening.

3) Is the school's office open

a) on Saturdays?   Yes   No   c) before 10.00 a.m. on Fridays?   Yes   No

b) on Fridays?   Yes   No   d) after 6.00 p.m. on Wednesdays?   Yes   No

4) When should you phone again?

a) between 9.30–12.00 on Saturday ☐   c) before 17.30 any weekday ☐

b) after 9.30 any weekday ☐

Discriminate and eliminate

Look at these three posters for the Oxbridge School of English. One is correct. The other two contain mistakes. Listen to Part A of the tape again to find out which poster is correct.

5)

a)
The
Oxbridge School
Of English

4 Blackwell Lane, Oxford
Tel: Oxford 876942
Mon-Fri 09.30–17.30

b)
The
Oxbridge School
Of English

206 Tring Road, Oxbridge
Tel: Oxbridge 876942
Mon-Fri 09.30–17.00
24 hour answering machine service

c)
The
Oxbridge School
Of English

162 Bristol Street, Oxbridge
Tel: Oxbridge 876942
Mon-Fri 09.30–17.30
24 hour answering machine service

PART **B**

Intensive listening

While you were out a friend telephoned and left a message on your answering machine. Read question 6, then listen to Part B of the tape. Answer while you are listening.

6) Which of these sentences are true (T) and which are false (F)?

a) Irene phoned while you were out. ☐
b) Eileen phoned while you were out. ☐
c) She has two tickets for the ballet. ☐
d) She has two tickets for *Othello*. ☐
e) Irene can't go to the opera. ☐
f) The opera starts at 19.00. ☐
g) Irene is taking Harry to the dentist tomorrow. ☐
h) Irene is taking Harry to the dentist tomorrow before 10.00 a.m. ☐

Discriminate and eliminate

Look at these pairs of tickets. One pair is Irene's. Listen to Part B of the tape again to find out which pair is hers.

7)

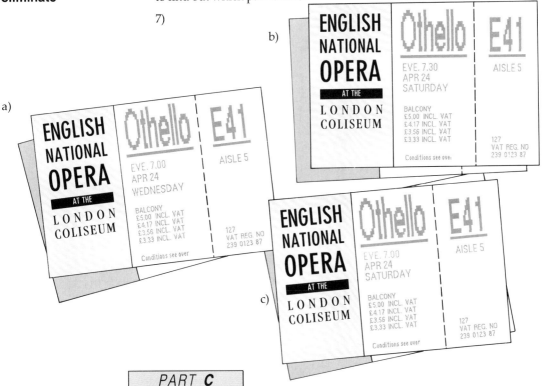

PART **C**

Additional activities: Vocabulary and fluency

8) Write a short message for your own answering machine.

9) Who do you think Rodney and Harry are (Part B)?

UNIT 2   'So you wanna keep fit, huh?'

Pre-listening discussion questions

Crystal Collins's new book tells you how to get fit and stay healthy. It's easy, and it only takes a few minutes each day.

1) Do you take any form of regular, physical exercise? If so, what, and why? If not, why not?
2) How important is good health to you? What are the best ways of keeping fit and healthy? Do you have any tips?
3) Have you ever bought a book of keep fit exercises? If so, why, and do you still use it?

PART A

Intensive listening

There's a cassette with Crystal Collins's new book. In it she describes lots of physical exercises. But you have to be careful. Read question 1 and then listen to Part A of the tape. Answer while you are listening.

1) Which of these are Crystal's five 'golden rules'?

a) Everybody should take physical exercise. ☐
b) Wear comfortable clothes. ☐
c) Don't eat too much too quickly. ☐
d) Don't smoke. ☐
e) Do warming-up exercises before you begin. ☐
f) Don't try too much exercise too soon. ☐
g) Everybody needs exercise. ☐
h) Take it easy for a few minutes after exercise. ☐
i) Everybody wants to keep fit. ☐
j) Always stop if you feel unwell. ☐

Physical exercise

Now do this warming-up exercise from Crystal Collins's new book:

A simple warming-up routine

1 Jog gently, on the spot, for 15 seconds. Lift your feet at least 10 cm.

2 Now stand with your feet apart. Rest your hands on your hips. Gently bend to the left, then to the right. Move gently. Avoid short, sharp movements. Do this for 30 seconds.

PART B

Vocabulary: Parts of the body

2) Write words from this list next to the appropriate parts of the body, on this diagram:

ankle	chin	lungs
armpit	elbow	stomach
cheek	forehead	throat
chest	knuckles	wrist
legs	feet	

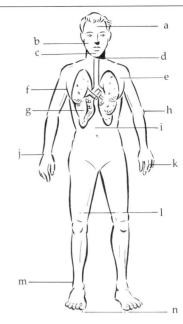

Listening for specific words

Read activity 3. Now listen to Part B of the tape, and do activity 3 while you are listening.

3) Circle on the diagram above all the parts of the body you hear.

Following instructions

Read the instructions for activity 4 and then listen to Part B of the tape again. Do activity 4 while you are listening.

4) Listen to Crystal's instructions very carefully. Do the physical exercise. You will need a strong chair.

Writing instructions

Look at these diagrams. Study them carefully, and then do exercise 5.

5) a) Stand with your ....

b) Raise your right ....

c) Make a circle above ....

d) Repeat ....

e) Now do it with ....

PART C

Additional activities: Instructions and discussion

6) Write and record some keep fit exercises for the class. Then start each lesson with five minutes of warming-up and keep fit exercises.

7) What do you think are the five best ways of keeping fit and healthy? Design a 'healthy living' programme for yourself.

UNIT 3 Inter-City 125

On many trains the guard makes announcements during the journey. He announces the names of the stations where the train will stop. There are sometimes announcements about where and when you can buy food on the train. You need to understand these if you don't want to get lost or be hungry!

Pre-listening discussion questions

1) Have you ever made a long journey by train in a foreign country? Were you nervous? What things, if any, worried you most?
2) What can you learn about a country from its railways?
3) Where would you most like to travel by train, and why?

PART A

Listening for specific information

Read questions 1 and 2 and then listen to Part A of the tape. Answer while you are listening.

1) What time does the train leave Edinburgh? _____
2) What time should it arrive in London? _____

Listening for place names

Study the map and read activity 3. Then listen to Part A of the tape again and do activity 3 while you are listening.

3) Draw the train's route on the map and write down the names of the stations where you should change trains if you are going to:

a) Sunderland: change at _____

b) Teesside Airport: change at _____

c) Scarborough: change at _____

PART B

Listening for detail

Read activity 4 and then listen to Part B of the tape. Do activity 4 while you are listening.

4) Write a tick (√) next to the things you can buy in the buffet car:

Drinks

Tea ☐   Cola ☐   Hot chocolate ☐
Beer ☐   Spirits ☐   Wines ☐
Coffee ☐   Lemonade ☐

Sandwiches

Egg and tomato ☐   Ham and tomato ☐   Egg and chips ☐
Roast chicken ☐   Toasted chicken ☐   Chicken and cheese ☐

Hot food

Cheeseburgers ☐   Fishburgers ☐   Sausage and chips ☐

PART C

Listening for gist and making inferences

Read question 5 and then listen to Part C of the tape. Then listen to Parts B and C together, without a break, and make brief notes while listening, if you want to. Then answer question 5.

5) What are the differences between the buffet car and the restaurant car. Try to think of at least three differences.

a) _____

b) _____

c) _____

PART D

Additional activities: Discussion and project work

6) Here's a sign you probably haven't seen before. What do you think it means? Would you like to see such a sign introduced? If so, where?

7) Use a good world atlas to plan your dream railway journey. Include stopovers and excursions and estimate how long your journey could take and how much it might cost.

UNIT 4 | Bibi Khanym and the Origin of the Muslim Veil

The mosque of Bibi Khanym is one of the most beautiful buildings in Samarkand. Bibi Khanym was the favourite wife of King Tamerlane. The legend of her mosque is said to explain why Muslim women wear a veil over their face.

Pre-listening discussion questions

1) Do you know any stories which explain natural or historical phenomena (such as how the elephant got its trunk, why ships are launched with a bottle of champagne or why a rabbit's foot is said to be lucky)? Tell any story like this that you know.
2) Which places in the world would you most like to visit, and why? Do some places have magical, exotic names for you? Which places? Are they exotic to everyone? Why do they sound so exotic to some people?
3) Where, exactly, is Samarkand?

PART A

Listening for gist

Read exercise 1 and then listen to the tape. Complete exercise 1 after you have listened.

1) Complete this sentence:

According to King Tamerlane, a woman's beauty can be _____.

Listening for specific information

Read exercise 2 and then listen to the tape again. Answer while you are listening.

2) A student wrote these notes while she was listening to the tape. Unfortunately, she made a few mistakes. Underline her mistakes.

> 7th century – Central Africa – powerful soldier – great empire – Atlantic to Indian Ocean – capital mountain city Samarkand – many mosques – blue ceramic tiles inside – gold outside.
>
> T. had many wives – favourite Arab girl – B.K. – most beautiful – oldest most important wife.
>
> B.K. decided build mosque – found architect – work started immediately.
>
> B.K. fell in love with master builder – mosque finished – T. returns home – killed B.K. and builder – Muslim women wear veil in memory of B.K.

Now read question 3 and then listen to the tape again, if you need to. Answer while you are listening.

3) Which of these sentences are true (T) and which are false (F)?

a) Tamerlane was a warrior. ☐
b) Samarkand was surrounded by desert. ☐
c) The mosques were decorated with gold inside. ☐
d) Bibi Khanym was Tamerlane's chief wife. ☐
e) Bibi Khanym designed the mosque herself, to honour her husband. ☐
f) The master builder fell in love with Bibi Khanym as soon as he first saw her. ☐
g) The master builder agreed to finish the mosque if Bibi Khanym would let him kiss her once. ☐
h) Bibi Khanym loved the master builder more than anything else. ☐
i) Tamerlane returned unexpectedly. ☐
j) The architect was killed by Tamerlane. ☐

PART B

Additional activities: Speculation and story-telling.

4) How do you think Bibi Khanym spent the rest of her life?

5) Record a story you know and exchange your recording with another student. Listen to his/her recording and make notes of questions you will ask later.

UNIT 5 Who's who?

When a new English course starts, the teacher sometimes asks the students to introduce themselves to the rest of the class. It's a good way to get to know each other quickly.

Pre-listening discussion questions

1) How would you describe what Mr Gorbachev looks like? The Queen? The 'Mona Lisa'? The Statue of Liberty?
2) Describe your room, house/apartment, office, birthplace, favourite place or favourite childhood toy.
3) Describe your wife/husband, girl/boyfriend, best friend, heroine/hero, parent(s), pet(s).

PART A

Listening to identify people

Read exercise 1 and then listen to Part A of the tape. Complete the exercise while you are listening.

1) Three students are introducing themselves to the rest of the class. Look at the class photo and identify the three students you hear. Write their names and the countries they come from, below:

a) _____ from _____
b) _____ from _____
c) _____ from _____

1   2   3   4   5   6   7   8

Now read exercise 2 and then listen to Part A of the tape again. Complete the exercise while you are listening.

2) Which of these sentences are true (T) and which are false (F)?

a) Göran is from Scandinavia. ☐
b) He has been studying in Britain during the summer. ☐
c) He is blond. ☐
d) People often expect Swedes to be tall and blond. ☐
e) Most Swedes like sailing and skiing. ☐
f) The old name for Sri Lanka was Ceylon. ☐
g) Shanti doesn't speak Tamil at home in India. ☐
h) She's a medical student in Britain. ☐
i) Michel thinks his English is rather good. ☐
j) He is very relaxed. ☐

PART B

Intensive listening: Physical descriptions

There have been several bank and post office robberies recently. The police are investigating the crimes and they would like to interview two men and one woman who were seen near two of the banks last week. Read activity 3, then listen to Part B of the tape. Do the activity while you are listening.

3) A police officer is describing to journalists at a press conference the three people they would like to interview. Use the information you hear to help you to complete these drawings of the three people.

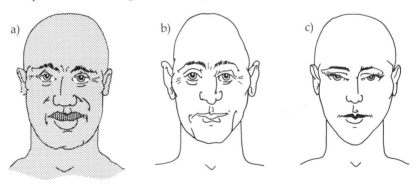

PART C

Additional activities: Introduction and description

4) Look at the photograph in exercise 1 again. Choose one of the students in the picture and prepare a short introduction for him/her. Present your introduction to the class as though you were that student.

5) Describe a picture or photograph to someone who hasn't seen it. Get him/her to draw the picture or to describe it (without seeing it) to another student. The third student should then describe the picture to you. How accurate is the description?

UNIT 6 Radio Advertisements

Commercial radio stations are partly financed by advertising. Some people think that the adverts are better than the programmes!

Pre-listening discussion questions

1) Do you ever listen to a local English language commercial radio station? Does it help you with your English? How/Why not?
2) Can you think of any new words or expressions you've learned from the radio?
3) Do you listen to the advertisements and announcements or just the programmes? Why? Have you got a favourite radio, TV or cinema advert? If you have, what is it, and why do you like it so much?

PART A

Listening for specific information: Sound discrimination

In Part A you will hear three advertisements. Read exercise 1 and then listen to Part A of the tape. Do the exercise while you are listening.

1) a) Tick (√) the names of the companies or products you hear:

Simple Saver supermarket ☐	*Freda* women's magazine ☐
Simply Sofabeds ☐	One Step Music Centre ☐
Freedom women's magazine ☐	Wanstead Music Centre ☐
Leader women's magazine ☐	Wanstead Piano Centre ☐
Prima women's magazine ☐	Just Pianos ☐

b) Tick the types of product you hear:

food ☐	synthesisers ☐	
clothes ☐	pianos ☐	
furniture ☐	records and cassettes ☐	
magazine ☐		

Intensive listening for detail

Now read exercise 2, then listen to Part A of the tape again. Complete the exercise while you are listening.

2) Fill in the missing information below:

a) The address of Simply Sofabeds: _____ Notting Hill Gate

b) The price of *Prima*: _____

c) The telephone number of the Wanstead Music Centre: _____

Extensive listening

Read questions 3 to 5 and then listen to Part A of the tape a third time. Answer after you have listened.

3) Why are they lowering their prices at Simply Sofabeds?

4) Is *Prima* a new magazine? How do you know?

5) Does the Wanstead Music Centre sell other musical instruments beside pianos?

PART B

Listening for specific information: Sound discrimination and extensive listening for detail

In Part B you will hear five advertisements. Read exercise 6 and then listen to the tape. Do the exercise while you are listening.

6) You will hear advertisements for a) a magazine, b) a soap, c) a radio programme, d) a washing powder, and e) an office design service. Tick the names of the companies or products you hear:

a) i) *Car Buyer* magazine ☐
    ii) *Car Hire* magazine ☐

b) i) Cuticura medicated soap ☐
    ii) Cute and Curly medicated soap ☐
    iii) Cute and Cheerful medicated soap ☐

c) i) Pop News ☐
    ii) The Bob Harris Music Show ☐
    iii) LBC Pop Review ☐
    iv) BBC Pop Review ☐

d) i) A real automatic washing powder ☐
    ii) Area automatic washing powder ☐
    iii) Ariel automatic washing powder ☐
    iv) Arium automatic washing powder ☐

e) i) Shift Interiors ☐
    ii) Swift Interiors ☐
    iii) Sniffed Interiors ☐
    iv) Stiffed Interiors ☐

Now read exercise 7, then listen to Part B of the tape again. Complete the exercise while you are listening.

7) Fill in the missing information below:

a) The price of *Car Buyer* is _____.

b) You can buy Cuticura soap from _____.

c) Bob Harris's radio programme starts at _____.

d) Jill Lancaster recently bought a Servis _____ washing machine.

e) The phone number of Swift Interiors is _____.

PART C

Additional activities: Writing and vocabulary work

8) Study this advert from a magazine and then write, produce and record a one-minute radio advertisement for the restaurant.

The Beehive Restaurant.
Everything you thought vegetarian food couldn't be.

The Beehive. 11a Beehive Place, (off Brixton Station Road) London, SW9 7QR 01-274-1690.

9) Read the tapescript for this Unit (page 52). Make a list of any words or expressions you didn't know. Then exchange lists with a partner. Try to explain the words and expressions on each list to each other. Discuss any difficulties you have with other pairs of students.

| UNIT 7 | # Terminal One |

At airports it's often difficult to hear the announcements. Even when you can hear them it's not always easy to understand them.

Pre-listening discussion questions

1) Write a list of about 10–15 adjectives which describe your opinion of air travel.
2) Have you ever flown first or business class? What are the differences between first class and 'tourist' class?
3) How do you feel about airports? Are they generally exciting, sad, stressful, beautiful, intimate, dangerous, hot, welcoming . . . ?

PART A

Listening for specific information

Study the map and read exercise 1. Then listen to the tape. Complete exercise 1 while you are listening.

1) Underline the names of all the places you hear.

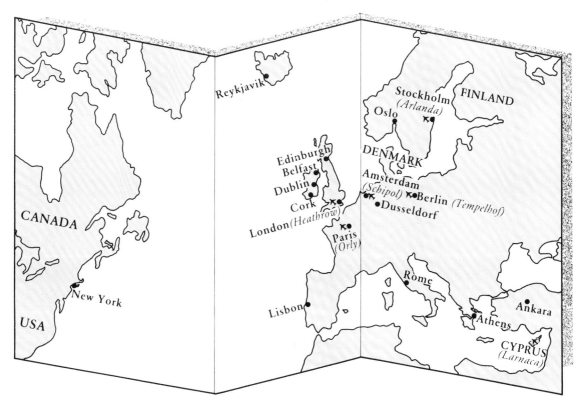

Now complete exercise 2.

2) Match the symbols with the correct words:
checking in   boarding   closing

a)    b)   c)

Read exercise 3 and then listen to the tape again. Do the exercise while you are listening.

3) Fill in the missing information on this departures board.

Destination	Flight No.	Gate No.	Flight information
Edinburgh	Super Shuttle		Boarding
	BA 838		Checking in
Dublin		6	
Athens			

Now read exercise 4. Listen to the tape a third time and complete the table while you are listening.

4) Fill in the missing information about the passengers:

Title	Forename	Surname	Travel information
Mr	Ian	Jackman	recently arrived from _____
Dr	Raymond	_____	from _____
Ms	Yvonne	Simpson	from _____
____		Waring	meeting _____
Capt.	Jay	Brock	from _____
Mr	_____	Sandberg	_____
____	Margaret	Murphy	in transit from _____ to _____

PART B

Additional activities: Brainstorming and inventing stories

5) What features should the ideal airport have? Work in large groups and brainstorm your ideas. Brainstorming means everyone contributes their ideas and all the ideas are written on the board. There must be no evaluation of the ideas until the contributions stop. Then discuss the ideas and decide which to keep and which to discard.

6) You have just arrived at the international airport in Tirana, the capital of Albania, in the Balkans. It is around midnight. When you get through passport control and customs you discover that the person who was going to meet you is nowhere in sight. In fact, the airport is deserted. After a few minutes a young woman approaches you, gives you this note and disappears:

Explain the note to a partner. What has happened? Who is 'S'? What will you do now? Why did you fly to Tirana? What do you do for a living? Where did you fly from? Be imaginative!

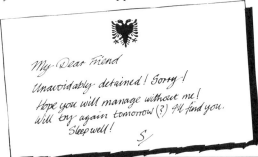

My Dear Friend
Unavoidably detained! Sorry!
Hope you will manage without me!
Will try again tomorrow (?) I'll find you.
Sleep well!
S/

UNIT 8 — The Touch of Death

This short story is about a teenage girl, Sally, who is about to leave home. It is based on an original idea by Dawn Hunt.

Pre-listening discussion questions

1) What sort of stories do you prefer – happy or sad? romantic or violent? science-fiction or historical? Why?
2) Do you have a favourite story from childhood? If so, what is it? How much of it can you remember?
3) Do you like stories for adults about childhood and adolescence?

PART A

Extensive listening to identify mood and personality

Read questions 1 and 2 and then listen to the tape. Choose your answers to both questions after you have listened.

1) Which of these sentences best describes Sally?

   a) She is a 25-year-old university student. ☐
   b) She is very excited about leaving home and is looking forward to it. ☐
   c) She is a little nervous about leaving home. ☐
   d) She is extremely homesick. ☐
   e) She is worried about her plants and her goldfish. ☐

2) Which of these sentences best describes Sally's mother?

   a) She is very proud of her daughter. ☐   d) She is unhappy. ☐
   b) She is absent-minded. ☐   e) She is a widow. ☐
   c) She is extremely happy. ☐

Listening for specific information

Read questions 3 to 5 and then listen to the tape again. Answer as many of the questions as you can while you are listening. Play the tape a third time if you need to.

3) a) How old is Sally?
   b) What's her surname?
   c) What's her parents' phone number?

4) Which two things does Sally's mother agree to look after?

   a) her furniture and curtains ☐ c) her plants and goldfish ☐
   b) her clothes and puppy ☐   d) her father and brother ☐

5) Who or what died?

   a) her mother ☐   d) her father ☐
   b) her puppy ☐   e) her plants ☐
   c) her goldfish ☐

Read question 6 and then listen to the story again. Answer while you are listening.

6) In the story, which of these sentences are true (T) and which are false (F)?

   a) Sally had always lived with her parents. ☐
   b) They lived in Yorkshire. ☐
   c) Sally had bought furniture and curtains for her new home. ☐
   d) Sally's mother had promised to send her some furniture. ☐
   e) Sally's college was a long way from her parents' home. ☐

PART B

Additional activities: Dialogue and discussion

7) a) What do you think Sally's mother said in reply to Sally's question about her father?
   b) Continue the story. Write the next six lines of dialogue between Sally and her mother.

8) What sort of man do you think Sally's father is or was? Discuss this with a partner, then write a brief description of him.

9) What three things worried or worry you most about leaving home? What three things did you look forward to or are you looking forward to about leaving home?

UNIT 9 Dial-A-Recipe: Chilled Paprika Chicken

In Britain, the United States and several other countries, the telephone company provides services such as Dial-A-Record, the Speaking Clock and daily weather and travel reports.

Pre-listening discussion questions

1) How useful do you think telephone services such as Dial-A-Joke or Dial-A-Prayer are? Are there any telephone services which are essential?
2) What do you think people eat in the United States, Australia, India, Japan?
3) Who does most/all of the cooking where you live? Why?

PART A

Intensive listening for specific information

Chris has dialled the Dial-A-Recipe number. He has a pencil and paper ready and is waiting to write down today's recipe. Read exercise 1 and then listen to Part A of the tape. Complete exercise 1 while you are listening.

1) Fill in the missing information you hear.

```
  Kg cooked, skinned
                    mayonnaise
  ml
           soured
  1 tablespoonful paprika
    tablespoonfuls        puree
    teaspoonful caster sugar
    large, chopped, skinned

    freshly ground
```

PART B

Intensive listening for errors

Read through the completed recipe (in exercise 1) and then read the instructions for exercise 2. Listen to Part B of the tape and complete exercise 2 while you are listening.

2) When Chris wrote down the list of ingredients he made a few mistakes. Put a cross (×) in the column to the right of the recipe next to any item which Chris wrote down incorrectly. How many mistakes did he make and what were they?

PART C

Listening for key words

Read exercise 3 and then listen to Part C of the tape. Do the exercise while you are listening.

3) Write down how to make Chilled Paprika Chicken. Do not try to write complete sentences. Listen for the most important words – the key words – and write them in the spaces below. The first one is given as an example.

First, *remove bones*

Then, _____

Next, _____

Then, _____

Now, _____

Finally, _____

PART D

Intensive listening for errors

Read exercise 4 and study the recipe. Then listen to Part D of the tape and complete exercise 4 while you are listening.

4) Underline the mistakes in this recipe:

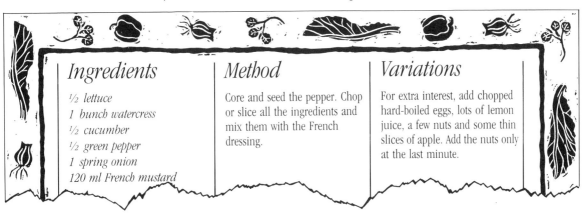

Ingredients
½ lettuce
1 bunch watercress
½ cucumber
½ green pepper
1 spring onion
120 ml French mustard

Method
Core and seed the pepper. Chop or slice all the ingredients and mix them with the French dressing.

Variations
For extra interest, add chopped hard-boiled eggs, lots of lemon juice, a few nuts and some thin slices of apple. Add the nuts only at the last minute.

PART E

Additional activities: Vocabulary and project work

5) Look at the verbs in list A and match them with suitable nouns from list B. There is more than one correct combination for several of the words.

A		B	
grated	shelled	grapefruit	olives
chopped	diced	chicken	cabbage
minced	stoned	apple	walnuts
cored	shredded	cod	celery
skinned	peeled	onion	cheese
boned		beef	tomato

6) Plan an English-speaking party for the class.

UNIT 10 — The Weather Forecast

Weather forecasting has become much more sophisticated in recent years. Satellites provide accurate and up-to-the-minute information about changes in the weather, and so weather forecasts are much more reliable than they used to be.

Pre-listening discussion questions

1) Do you ever read the weather forecast in your newspaper? Why/Why not?
2) Do you watch the weather forecast on TV more or less often than you listen to it on the radio? Why?
3) How would our lives be different if we had no weather forecasts?

PART A

Extensive listening

Read question 1 and then listen to Part A of the tape. Answer after you have listened.

1) What time of year do you think it might be, and what day of the week do you think it is, in the recording?

Intensive listening

Read question 2 and look at the four weather maps. Then listen to Part A of the tape again. Answer while you are listening.

2) Three of these weather maps are incorrect. Which is the correct one?

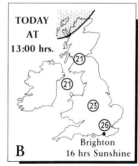
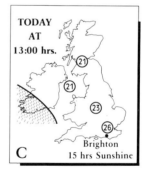

PART B

Intensive listening

Study the map and the weather symbols, then read exercise 3. Listen to Part B of the tape and do exercise 3 while you are listening (you may need to listen to Part B more than once in order to complete this exercise).

3) Draw the correct weather symbols in the appropriate places on this map.

Now read exercise 4. Then listen to Parts A and B of the tape together, without a pause. Do exercise 4 while you are listening.

4) Tick (✓) the correct ending for each of these sentences:

a) The weatherman's name is

i) Dan Francis ☐   ii) Stan Francis ☐   iii) Sam Francis ☐

b) He works at

i) London's Weather Centre ☐   iii) The London Weather Centre ☐

ii) The Weather Centre of London ☐

c) Tonight it will be mild and dry

i) everywhere ☐

ii) in most parts of the country ☐

iii) in south-east England and south Wales ☐

d) In Greece, this week-end, it's going to be

i) warm and sunny ☐   iii) warm with occasional showers ☐

ii) warm and overcast ☐

Vocabulary work

5) Match each word in the list on the left with a suitable definition from the list on the right:

a) occasional   i) quite warm
b) fine   ii) highest
c) settled   iii) dry
d) light   iv) lowest
e) reached   v) go away
f) mild   vi) became as high as
g) maximum   vii) not heavy
h) minimum   viii) forecast for the next few days
i) pass   ix) not changing much
j) outlook   x) sporadic

PART C

Additional activities: Time

6) The Radio Metro weather forecast, on the tape, was at two minutes to nine. Do you think that was 8.58 a.m. or 8.58 p.m.?

7) In English we don't usually say the word 'minutes' when we tell someone the time:
e.g. What time is it?   It's ten past two.

BUT
If the long hand is between the numerals on the clock, like this we say, 'It's two minutes past one.'   Now, what time is it?

a)   b) 04:17   c)   d) 01:15   e)

UNIT 11 | Buying a New Car

Monica and George have decided to buy a new car, but they haven't decided which one to buy. They've got brochures and price lists for five models and they're comparing them in order to make their final choice.

Pre-listening discussion questions

1) Have you ever bought a brand new car? If so, how did you decide which one to buy?
2) What can we tell about someone from the car she/he drives? What are the main influences when people choose cars? Is a car more than just a means of transport?
3) How would you feel about abolishing privately-owned cars and replacing them with pools of communally-owned cars where people could borrow a car when they could prove a genuine need for personal transport?

PART A

Intensive listening

1) Study the table and read exercise 1. Then listen to Part A of the tape and complete the table in exercise 1 while you are listening.

CAR	MG Metro		Peugeot 205	Renault 5	Ford Escort
MODEL	1300	GL			
ENGINE SIZE	1300 cc	1600 cc	cc	cc	cc
PRICE	£	£8090	£	£	£7182
PETROL CONSUMPTION	mpg	mpg		mpg	mpg
NUMBER OF DOORS					

Now read the five questions in exercise 2, then listen to Part A of the tape again. Answer while you are listening.

2) a) Was it George or Monica who suggested drawing up a list of advantages and disadvantages for each car?
   b) What's the maximum they can afford to spend?
   c) Why did they reject the Ford Escort?
   d) Does George like French cars?
   e) Which car did Monica think was George's favourite?

Speculating and discussing probability

Read question 3 and then listen to Part A of the tape again, if you need to. Answer after you have listened.

3) Which car do you think Monica and George finally bought, and why?

Vocabulary work

4) Use all the words in this list to label the drawing correctly:

f front bumper
rear bumper
headlamp
g rear light
h radiator grille
i bonnet
aerial
mud flap
wing mirror
j windscreen wiper

Extensive listening: Identifying attitudes

Listen to Part A of the tape again, if you need to, then answer question 5.

5) Is George or Monica more enthusiastic about buying a new car?

PART B

Listening for specific information

You will hear part of a radio consumer report programme. A car has been tested and the reporter is explaining some of the problems she found. Read exercise 6 and then listen to Part B of the tape. Do the exercise while you are listening.

6) Mark with a cross (×) on the drawing on the left the parts of the car where there were problems.

Vocabulary work

7) Match each of the words in the list on the left with a suitable definition from the list on the right:

a) overpriced   i) covered, so as to reduce heat loss or noise
b) slide   ii) a typical or noticeable quality or characteristic
c) feature   iii) to change or alter something so as to make it more suitable or more comfortable
d) insulated   iv) costing more than you think it should, or more than it's worth
e) adjust   v) move smoothly

PART C

Additional activities: Making comparisons and stating priorities

8) Look again at the information in the table in exercise 1. Which car would *you* choose? Why? Give two reasons for not choosing each of the others.

9) What, for you, are the five most important features of a car? Select features from this list or add ideas of your own:

a) modern appearance   g) reliability
b) powerful engine   h) cheap spare parts
c) safety features   i) large luggage space
d) rust resistant   j) good radio-cassette player
e) colour   k) low petrol consumption
f) comfort   l) exclusive image

UNIT 12 — The London Marathon

The first London Marathon was run in 1981. It was a huge success and now over 20,000 runners take part in it every year.

Pre-listening discussion questions

1) Has anyone in your class ever taken part in a marathon/half marathon/any kind of endurance sporting event? If so, why did she/he do it? If not, why not?
2) Why is jogging so popular? Do you ever jog? If so, why? What do you get out of it? If not, why not? Do you do any other sport or physical exercise instead?
3) Do you have any unfulfilled ambition(s) in sport? If so, what are they? Do you think you'll ever fulfil your ambition?

PART A

Extensive listening

Rob Jackson is talking about his experience of running in the London Marathon. Read question 1 and then listen to the tape. Answer after you have listened, but make any brief notes you want to make while you are listening.

1) Which of these words best describes how Rob Jackson feels about having finished a London Marathon?

a) exhausted ☐   d) cheerful ☐
b) proud ☐   e) regretful ☐
c) worried ☐

Intensive listening: Following directions

Now study the map. Read activity 2 and then listen to the tape again. Complete activity 2 while you are listening.

2) Mark the race route on this map.

THE LONDON MARATHON

[Map of the London Marathon route showing landmarks including: The Monument, Queen Victoria St, Leadenhall St, Commercial Road, Stepney, Burdett Road, Leman St, East Rd, The Tower of London, Cable St, The Highway, Blackfriars Underpass, Northumberland Ave, The Strand, Blackfriars Br, Lower Thames St, St. Katherines Dock, East India Dock Road, Blackwall Tunnel, Thames Barrier, Admiralty Arch, Victoria Embankment, York Rd, Southwark St, Tower Bridge, Rotherhithe St, Westferry Road, Pall Mall, The Mall, Whitehall, Westminster Bridge, Jamaica Road, Surrey Docks, Lower Road, Redriff Road, Isle of Dogs, Bugsbys Way, Woolwich Church St, Wilton, Buckingham Palace, Birdcage Walk, The Finish, Druid St, Blackwall La, Woolwich Road, Charlton La, ROUTES MERGE, Little Heath, Big Ben, New Kent Road, Tower Bridge Rd, Old Kent Road, Rotherhithe New Road, Evelyn Road, Creek St, Romney Road, Cutty Sark, Charlton Road, Charlton Park Lane, Deptford Church St, Greenwich Park, Red Start, St. John's Park, New Cross Rd, Elite Women & WCC & RRA Start, Shooters Hill Road, Blue Start]

32

Read exercise 3 and study the table, below. Listen to the tape a third time and complete exercise 3 while you are listening.

3) Fill in the missing information on this table of previous winners:

PREVIOUS WINNERS OF THE LONDON MARATHON				
YEAR	MEN	COUNTRY	WOMEN	COUNTRY
1981	Inge Simonsen Dick Beardsley	USA	Joyce Smith	_____
1982	Hugh Jones	_____	_____	_____
1983	Mike Gratton	_____	Greta Waitz	_____
1984	Charlie Spedding	_____	Ingrid Kristiansen	_____
1985	Steve Jones	_____	_____	_____

You can listen to the tape a fourth time and complete exercise 4 while you are listening, or you can try it without listening again. To check your answers, though, you should listen once more after you have finished the exercise.

4) Complete these sentences by choosing the correct preposition to fill the space:
a) In John Wilson Street the elite runners joined _____ everyone else.
    i) to   iii) with
    ii) on   iv) by

b) Tower Bridge is just _____ the top of Jamaica Road.
    i) in   iii) at
    ii) on   iv) with

c) The second time, you go _____ Tower Bridge.
    i) on   iii) across
    ii) through   iv) under

d) Then you run _____ the underpass.
    i) in   iii) by
    ii) through   iv) on

e) You turn left _____ Birdcage Walk.
    i) into   iii) with
    ii) across   iv) on

PART B

**Additional activities:
Giving directions and planning a route**

5) Work with a large-scale city street map. Design a jogging route which you think will be pleasant, safe, healthy, convenient and not too difficult. Then describe your route to a partner who should follow it on the map.

UNIT 13

The People's Republic of China: Facts and Figures

In this Unit you will hear two extracts from a radio documentary programme about life in modern China.

Pre-listening discussion questions

1) What do you know about China?
2) What sort of people do you think the modern Chinese are? Do you think they have any unique national characteristics – or are most people around the world more or less similar?
3) Would you like to visit China? Why/Why not? Would it be better to visit China as a tourist or to work there for a while? Why?

PART A

Listening for gist

Read question 1 and then listen to Part A of the tape. Choose your answer while you are listening.

1) Has Part A of the tape been taken from

a) the beginning ☐   b) the middle ☐   c) the end ☐

of the radio programme? Tick (√) the correct answer.

Listening for specific information

Read questions 2 to 4, then listen to Part A of the tape again. Answer while you are listening.

2) China is the world's oldest surviving civilisation. How long is its history?
3) China is the third largest country in the world. Which two countries are larger?
4) China has the largest population of any country in the world. Approximately, how many people live there?

Study the map below, and read activity 5. Then listen to Part A of the tape again. Complete the activity while you are listening. You may need a little time after the extract has ended, to finish writing.

5) These states all share a border with the People's Republic of China:
North Korea,
The USSR,
Mongolia,
Afghanistan,
Pakistan,
India,
Nepal,
Sikkim,
Bhutan,
Burma,
Laos,
Vietnam.
Write down the names of the missing countries on this map.

34

PART B

Extensive listening

Read question 6 then listen to Part B of the tape. Choose your answer after you have listened.

6) Which of the following titles best summarises the extract?

a) China Today ☐   c) China – Land and Population ☐
b) The Land of a Billion Mouths ☐   d) China's Gifts to the World ☐

Listening for specific information

Read questions 7 to 9 then listen to Part B of the tape again. Answer while you are listening.

7) Which of the following inventions are not mentioned on the tape?

a) paper ☐   b) fireworks ☐   c) silk ☐   d) suntan oil ☐

8) What, approximately, is the size of the total land area of China? _____

9) What percentage of the Chinese population live in cities? _____

China has more than 12 cities with two million inhabitants. Look at the bar graph in question 10 then listen to Part B of the tape again. Do question 10 while you are listening. You may need a little time after the extract has ended, to finish writing.

10) Fill in the missing information on this bar graph:

A City: _____
Population: 12,000,000
B City: Beijing/Peking
Population: _____
C City: Tianjin
Population: _____
D City: Chonqing
Population: _____

PART C

Additional activities: Words and numbers

11) Match each of these words with a suitable definition:

a) surviving   i) owns or uses jointly or together with others
b) population   ii) continuing; still living or existing
c) inhabitants   iii) part or piece
d) extract (n)   iv) the people who live in a place
e) shares (v)   v) the number of people living in an area or country

12) Write these figures in words:

a) 28,072 km _____

b) 6,250 km^2 _____

c) 21% _____

d) $\frac{1}{3}$ _____

e) $\frac{1}{4}$ _____

UNIT 14 — A Valuable Collection?

Andrew Simpson collects badges and has just written a book about his hobby. He's being interviewed by a journalist. You will hear him talking about how he first became interested in badges.

Pre-listening discussion questions

1) Why do people wear badges? What different sorts, or categories, of badge can you think of?

2) What sort of people do you think might wear each of these badges?
3) Why do some people collect badges? Are some people 'natural' collectors? Are women less likely to collect things than men? How might a badge collection become valuable?

PART A

Extensive listening

Read question 1 and then listen to Part A of the tape. Answer while you are listening.

1) When do you think Andrew Simpson was born?

a) in the early 1900s ☐   c) in the early 1950s ☐
b) between 1940–45 ☐   d) after 1955 ☐

Listening for specific information

Read questions 2 to 4 and then listen to Part A of the tape again. Answer while you are listening.

2) What colour was the 'Tidy' badge?

a) blue ☐   c) yellow ☐
b) green ☐   d) red ☐

3) Which badge does Andrew Simpson think he has lost?

a) 'Swimming' ☐   c) A petrol company badge ☐
b) 'Wills's Woodbines' ☐   d) 'Tidy' ☐

4) What is the slogan on the Wills's Woodbines badge?

a) 'Loved by Millions' ☐   c) 'Smoked by the Million' ☐
b) 'Bought by Millions' ☐   d) 'Smoked by Millions' ☐

PART B

Listening for gist

Read question 5 and then listen to Part B of the tape. Answer after you have listened.

5) Which of the following best summarises Part B?

a) Badges from Eastern Europe ☐   c) Reasons for collecting badges ☐
b) Political badges ☐   d) Why people wear badges ☐

Intensive listening

Andrew Simpson gives three main reasons why people wear badges. Read exercise 6 and study the table, below. Then listen to Part B of the tape again and do the exercise while you are listening.

6) Tick (✓) the three reasons Andrew Simpson gives to explain why people wear badges:

First reason	Second reason	Third reason
People wear badges because . . .	People wear badges to . . .	People wear badges from . . .
a) . . . they like badges ☐	a) . . . express a message ☐	a) . . . their cars ☐
b) . . . they collect them ☐	b) . . . attract attention ☐	b) . . . America ☐
c) . . . they belong to a club ☐	c) . . . hide holes in their clothes ☐	c) . . . their club, trade union or political party ☐
d) . . . badges are cheap ☐	d) . . . advertise products ☐	d) . . . places they've visited ☐

PART C

Extensive listening

Read question 7 then listen to Part C of the tape. Answer after you have listened.

7) Is Andrew Simpson's collection worth a lot of money?

PART D

Additional activities: Design projects

8) Design a badge for the institution where you are studying English.

9) Design a badge which tourists would want to buy if they visited your town or city.

UNIT 15 What's in a Name?

William Shakespeare wrote that 'a rose by any other name would smell just as sweet'. But would it, really? Don't the names of things affect the way we respond to them?

Pre-listening discussion questions

1) What's the name of your favourite soap, shampoo or toothpaste? Why do you prefer these brands? Would you buy the same products if their names were changed to 'Yuk', 'Greeze' and 'Slime'?
2) Do you think that a camera called the 'Ambassador' would be more or less expensive than one called the 'Trudi'? Is one of these cameras for women and one for men? How do you know?
3) Is 'Ambassador' a good name for a camera or not? Why/Why not?

PART A

Listening for names

Students at a New York business college are attending a lecture. The lecturer is a senior executive of one of America's leading advertising agencies and he's talking about the names of cars. Read exercise 1, then listen to the tape. Complete the exercise while you are listening.

1) Tick (✓) the car names you hear, on this list:

a) Volkswagen Golf ☐   f) (Ford) Sierra ☐
b) Rolls-Royce Silver Cloud ☐   g) (Bentley) Mulsanne ☐
c) (Triumph) Spitfire ☐   h) Fiat Panda ☐
d) Reliant Kitten ☐   i) Jaguar Sovereign ☐
e) Austin Cambridge ☐   j) Rover Sterling ☐

Read questions 2 to 4 then listen to the tape again.
Answer while you are listening.

2) Which of these cars was not made in the 1970s?

a) Maxi ☐   b) Herald ☐   c) Kadett ☐   d) Sierra ☐

3) Which of these cars is not a 'little city car'?

a) Nova ☐   b) Charade ☐   c) Mulsanne ☐   d) Polo ☐

4) Which of these is wrong?
A car with a number instead of a name seems

a) safer ☐   b) faster ☐   c) more reliable ☐   d) more advanced ☐

Extensive listening

Read question 5 and then listen to the tape once more. Answer after you have listened.

5) Complete the sentence by choosing the most accurate statement from the list:
According to the lecturer

a) big, powerful cars are more dangerous than small city cars. ☐

b) there were more road accidents in the 1960s than in the 1970s. ☐

c) motor car manufacturers began to use different types of names in the 1970s. ☐

d) all of today's cars have much more romantic names than in the past. ☐

PART B

Listening for specific information

J. R. Ackerley was an Englishman who went to India in 1923 as private secretary to the Maharajah of Chhokrapur. In 1932 he published a book about his Indian experiences called *Hindoo Holiday*. In Part B of the tape you will hear a very short extract from *Hindoo Holiday*. It describes how His Highness, the Maharajah chooses his cars. Read exercises 6 to 8 then listen to the tape. Listen twice if you need to, then complete the exercises.

6) Complete the sentence correctly.
The Maharajah bought a Sunbeam because

a) he was not really interested in cars. ☐
b) he knew nothing about cars. ☐
c) he already had a Moon. ☐
d) he thought it would be 'pretty'. ☐

7) Complete the sentence correctly.
The Maharajah

a) liked the Sunbeam. ☐
b) hated the Sunbeam. ☐
c) was disappointed by the Sunbeam. ☐
d) already had four Sunbeams. ☐

8) Complete the sentence correctly.
The Maharajah probably

a) didn't buy a Buick. ☐
b) already owned a Buick. ☐
c) liked the sound of the name, Buick. ☐
d) wanted a Buick. ☐

PART C

Additional activities: Words and meanings, and naming products

9) Read the tapescript for Part B of the tape (page 57) and find expressions or phrases in the text which mean
a) The Maharajah   d) think of
b) no different from e) obvious dislike
c) car name   f) talk about it

10) Invent a name for a new range of men's cosmetics. Then compare the name you have chosen/invented with the names chosen/invented by others in the class. Do they have anything in common?

UNIT 16 'Value for Money'

'Value for Money' is a consumer programme on the radio. Every week the 'Value for Money' team report on consumer goods they have tested.

Pre-listening discussion questions

1) If you are thinking about buying an expensive machine or domestic appliance, how do you decide which one to buy? Which of these is most likely to influence you: an advertisement in a magazine? the recommendation of a friend? a salesman or woman? a report in a consumer magazine? the attractiveness of its appearance? the price?
2) Do you ever watch or listen to consumer programmes? Why/Why not?
3) Do we rely too much on domestic appliances?

PART A

Listening for specific information

In this week's programme they're talking about coffee machines. Read questions 1 to 3 and then listen to the tape. Answer while you are listening.

1) How many machines did they test? _____

2) How much does the 'Kaffitalia' cost? _____

3) How long is the 'Domestika' guaranteed for? _____

Now look at these five information panels. Read exercise 4 and then listen to the tape again. Complete exercise 4 while you are listening.

3.50 Value for Money

Radio Metro's award-winning consumer programme returns with a new series. Janet Hill reports on a range of the latest coffee machines and Martin Hart interviews the managing director of Sunquest Holidays, Sir George Stenson, about the cut-price package tour war.

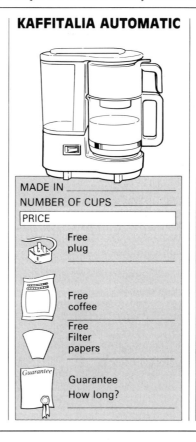

KAFFITALIA AUTOMATIC

MADE IN _____
NUMBER OF CUPS _____
PRICE

Free plug _____

Free coffee _____

Free Filter papers _____

Guarantee How long? _____

AROMACUP 2000

MADE IN _____
NUMBER OF CUPS _____
PRICE

Free plug _____

Free coffee _____

Free Filter papers _____

Guarantee How long? _____

4) Write the missing information in the correct spaces.

Study the information panels again, and then complete exercise 5.

5) Complete this sentence:

I think the _____ is the best coffee machine because _____

_____

_____

PART **B**

**Additional activities:
Naming products and
classroom survey**

6) Look at the names of the coffee machines again. Each name is designed so that
a) people remember it easily, and
b) it tells us what kind of machine it is (for example, 'Kaffematic' comes from *coffee* and *automatic*).
Think of good names for:
i) a new hair drier   ii) a new washing machine   iii) a new alarm clock

7) Carry out a classroom consumer report on wristwatches. Choose five students' watches and compare the prices, styles, materials used, functions, guarantees, etc., and try to decide which is the best value for money. Use the information you collect to write the script for another 'Value for Money' programme.

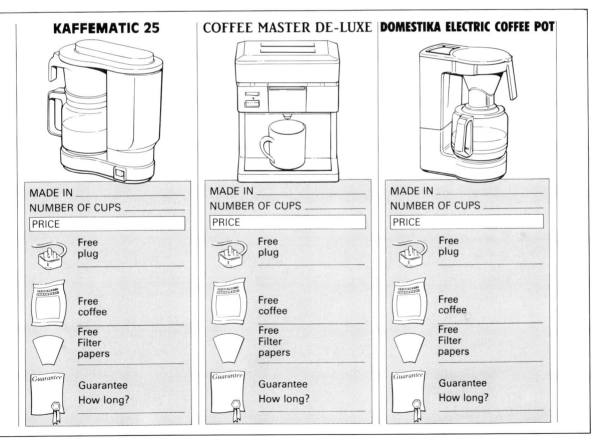

UNIT 17 | Programming the Video

Charlotte has a part-time job. She works five evenings a week as an usherette in her local cinema. She misses most of her favourite TV programmes, so she has decided to rent a video recorder.

Pre-listening discussion questions

1) Do you prefer to read the operating instructions for a machine from the instructions manual, or would you rather have someone explain and show you how to do it?
2) What's the most complicated piece of machinery you have ever learned to operate? What was the most difficult part to learn?
3) Do machines make life easier for us? Are some machines unnecessary or too complicated or too dangerous? Why do some people resist new technology?

PART A

Extensive listening: Recording a TV programme

At the video rental shop the assistant is explaining to Charlotte how to use the machine. Read question 1 and then listen to Part A of the tape. Choose your answer after you have listened.

1) Which of the following statements best summarises Part A of the tape?

a) The assistant is explaining to Charlotte how to programme the video. ☐
b) The assistant is explaining to Charlotte how to record a TV programme. ☐
c) Charlotte is asking the assistant how much a tape costs. ☐
d) The assistant is explaining to Charlotte how to operate the machine. ☐

Listening for specific information

Read questions 2 and 3 and then listen to Part A of the tape again. Answer while you are listening. You may need a little extra time to finish writing after Part A has finished.

2) What two things do you have to check before you record a TV programme?

3) When you want to record a TV programme, which two buttons do you have to press (once the machine is switched on) and which do you have to press first?

4) When you buy a video tape there is usually a sheet of self-adhesive labels inside the box. These labels are to help you identify the recordings you have made. There are usually blank labels, numbers, letters and symbols. Look at these symbols labels and match them with an appropriate text from the list on the right.

a)   e)
b)   f)
c)   g)
d)   h)

1 a children's programme or film
2 a current affairs or discussion programme
3 a home video
4 a recording of a rock or classical music concert
5 a feature film
6 a recording of the Italian Grand Prix
7 an educational programme
8 a film or TV production of a play

PART B

Listening for specific information: Programming the video I

Look at the diagram of Charlotte's video recorder, below. Read exercise 4 and then listen to Part B of the tape. Do exercise 5 while you are listening.

5) Write numbers in the circles to show the order in which you hear the buttons mentioned. The first one is done for you, as an example. If the STORE button is the next one you hear, write '2' in the circle connected to the STORE button, and so on.

Read question 6 then listen to Part B of the tape again. Answer while you are listening.

6) How many memory positions does Charlotte's VTR have? (NB: VTR stands for *Video Tape Recorder*.)

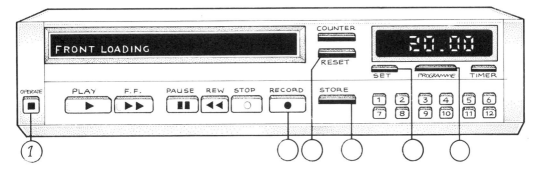

PART C

Listening for specific information: Programming the video II

Look at the information panel below. Then read exercise 7. Listen to Part C of the tape and do exercise 7 while you are listening.

7) a) Fill in the correct details to show how Charlotte's video has been programmed:

Channel selected _____ Day _____

Programme start time _____

Programme finish time _____

b) Which button do you have to press if you want to correct a programming mistake?

PART D

Additional activities: Giving instructions

8) Bring a small machine to class (e.g. camera, steam iron, food processor, digital watch, cassette player, combination lock briefcase, etc.) and explain to the rest of the class how to operate it.

9) Write a simple instructions leaflet for the machine you or another student brought to class.

UNIT 18 | The Department Store

Large department stores can be confusing. It's not always easy to find the department you're looking for. There's usually a store guide by each entrance, and there are often announcements to advertise special bargains and help shoppers find what they're looking for.

Pre-listening discussion questions

1) Is shopping basically pleasant or basically unpleasant?
2) Do you prefer small, specialist shops or larger department stores and supermarkets?
3) What do you especially like/dislike about department stores? Do you have a favourite shop or store in this town/city (or some other town/city)? What's so special about it for you?

PART A

Listening for specific information

1) Study the store guide to Bentley's department store, then read exercise 1. Listen to the tape and complete exercise 1 while you are listening.

FOURTH FLOOR
_____

THIRD FLOOR
Accounts
_____
Kitchen Design Service
Toilets

SECOND FLOOR
Bedding, Fabrics
Ladies' Shoes, Lingerie
_____
Towels

FIRST FLOOR
Children's Clothes
_____
Toys

GROUND FLOOR
_____ , _____
Leather Goods
'Manhattan' Boutique
Menswear, Stationery
Toilets

BASEMENT
Electrical goods
Furniture, Hardware
_____
Photographic

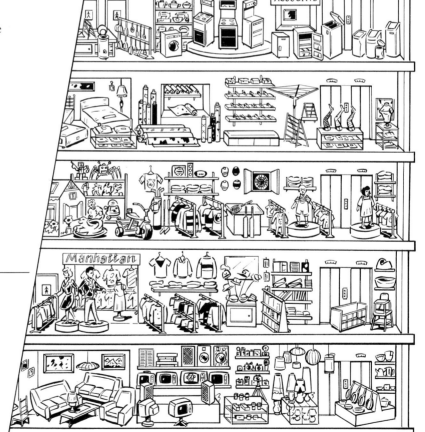

Read exercise 2 then listen to the tape again. Complete exercise 2 while you are listening.

2) Write down the prices you hear for each of the following:

a) Lambrusco (wine) £ _____ per bottle

b) 100% cotton sweaters from £ _____

c) Skirts from £ _____

d) Dunlop training shoes from £ _____

e) Track suits from £ _____

f) Tennis rackets from £ _____

Speculate

Read exercise 3 and then listen to the tape again. Do the exercise while you are listening and complete it after the recording has ended.

3) Which of these statements do you think are true and which do you think are false? It is important to note that while some of these are clearly either *true* or *false*, you will have to speculate about some of the others. Use the information you hear on the tape to help you decide.

a) Bentley's sell French swimsuits.
b) It's Italian Week in the 'Ritz' Boutique.
c) The 'Ritz' Boutique sells men's clothes.
d) Bentley's department store is air-conditioned.
e) The price of garden forks has been reduced by £3.50.
f) The Coffee Shop serves lunch.
g) The Customer Services Department is on the third floor.
h) The 100% cotton sweaters are for women.
i) The Coffee Shop serves snacks only.
j) You can get a free pair of gardening gloves in the Gardening Department.

Look at the store guide (exercise 1) again and complete exercise 4.

4) On which floor can you find the following?
a) ladies' underwear   d) curtain material
b) writing paper   e) pillow cases
c) cameras

PART B

Additional activities: Listing advantages and disadvantages and planning a department store

5) Write a list of the advantages of department stores, and another list of the disadvantages. Show your lists to two other students and discuss the differences between all your lists.

6) Plan a department store. Decide which departments your store will have, and discuss where each department should be placed. Write a store guide to show where you have decided to place each department.

UNIT 19 Radio Phone-In

Everyone has a personal problem at some time or other. It usually helps if you can talk to a friend about it. But that's not always possible. So 'Agony' columns in magazines and phone-in programmes on the radio are very popular.

Pre-listening discussion questions

1) Do your friends ever come to you with their problems? Do you think you are a good listener?
2) What qualities does a good listener need?
3) Why are 'agony' columns and problem phone-ins so popular?

PART A

Listening for gist

Rosemary's problem is her father. Read question 1 then listen to Part A of the tape. Answer after you have listened.

1) Which of these sentences best summarises the advice which Tessa and Maurice offer to Rosemary?
a) Listen to your father and try to understand his point of view.
b) You shouldn't really be out so late in such a dangerous city; your father is right.
c) Ask Christine's father to take you home once or twice a week.
d) Try to find a compromise.

Listening for specific information

Read exercise 2 then listen to Part A of the tape again. Do the exercise while you are listening.

2) Find out
a) how old Rosemary is _____
b) where she's from _____
c) her friend's name _____

PART B

Listening for gist

Jim is phoning from Glasgow. Read question 3 and then listen to Part B of the tape. Answer after you have listened.

3) Which of these sentences best summarises the advice Jim's doctor gave him?
a) Baldness is always passed on from father to son.
b) You should change your hairstyle.
c) Your baldness is probably unavoidable.
d) You should use a special shampoo.

Listening for specific information

Read exercise 4 and then listen to Part B of the tape again. Do the exercise while you are listening.

4) Find out

a) how old Jim is _____

b) what he asks Tessa and Maurice to recommend _____

c) whether they recommend one _____

PART C

Listening for specific information

Read questions 5 to 7 and then listen to Part C of the tape. Answer while you are listening.

5) How long has Martin been trying to stop smoking?

6) Does his girlfriend smoke?

7) Why did Martin start smoking again?
a) Because his girlfriend smokes.
b) Because his job is boring.
c) Because he likes cigarettes.
d) Because he says that smoking helps him when he's under pressure.

PART D

Additional activities: Giving advice

8) Write a letter giving advice to Martin.

9) Read this letter from the problem page of a family magazine, and then write a reply.

How do I find a reliable babysitter?

We've just moved to a new area with our two young children. My loneliness – I've left all my friends and family behind – is made worse because my husband and I never seem to go out together for want of someone to look after the children. Now with Christmas coming up we've had a few local invites which I'd really like to accept – it would be a great chance to meet people. But how do I find a reliable babysitter?

UNIT 20 — First Aid

Luo is a waiter in a restaurant in Hong Kong. In his spare time he is taking a correspondence course on Childcare. He wants to be a kindergarten assistant. Every week he receives a new home-study cassette and some reading. He has to complete one written assignment every month. This month the theme is first aid.

Pre-listening discussion questions

1) Have you ever studied first aid? If so, where, when and why? If not, would you say that a knowledge of first aid is useful?

2) Do you think that first aid should be a compulsory part of their training for all school teachers? Explain your reasons.

3) 'Natural' and 'alternative' medical treatment is always better than treatment which uses drugs. Do you agree or disagree with this?

PART A

Extensive listening

Read question 1 and then listen to the extract from Luo's home-study tape. Select your answer after you have listened.

1) Which of these is the best title for the extract?

a) First aid for young children. ☐
b) Cuts and grazes: a simple checklist. ☐
c) Dressing and cleaning cuts and grazes. ☐
d) How to stop serious bleeding. ☐

Intensive listening

Read questions 2 to 4 and then listen to the tape again. Answer while you are listening.

2) What should you do if a child is cut near the eye?

a) Dress the cut with a clean cotton bandage. ☐
b) Clean the cut with warm water. ☐
c) Hold the cut closed for a few minutes. ☐
d) Call a doctor. ☐

3) What should you do with a very deep cut?

a) Call a doctor as soon as possible. ☐
b) Press a piece of cotton wool firmly over the cut for about five minutes. ☐
c) Clean it and hold it closed with an adhesive dressing. ☐
d) Dress it with a clean cotton bandage. ☐

4) What should you do if the child is nervous or upset?

a) Give them a little water to drink. ☐   c) Let them rest quietly. ☐
b) Tell them a joke or a funny story. ☐   d) Call a doctor as soon as possible. ☐

Now look at the checklist diagram below, and read activity 5. Listen to the tape once more and complete activity 5 while you are listening.

5) Complete the diagram by filling in the missing words.

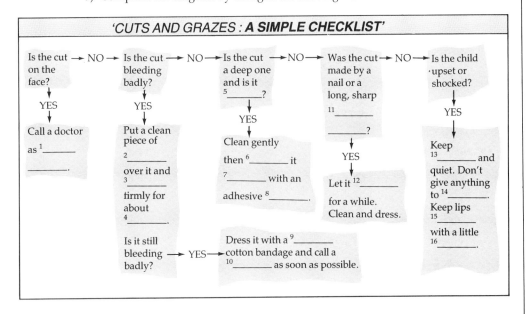

Vocabulary work

Read exercise 6. Listen to the tape a fourth time, if you need to. Then complete exercise 6.

6) Choose the correct definition for each of these words:

a) minor
  i) large ☐
  ii) unimportant ☐
  iii) serious ☐

b) grazes
  i) surface cuts ☐
  ii) accidents ☐
  iii) bleeding ☐

c) unavoidable
  i) very common ☐
  ii) preventable ☐
  iii) not preventable ☐

d) wound
  i) skin ☐
  ii) accident ☐
  iii) cut or tear ☐

PART B

Additional activities: Traditional remedies and compiling a first aid kit

7) What 'traditional' remedies do you know for common illnesses? What is the best thing to take for a cold? Do you know how to stop a nosebleed or what to rub into certain stings? Work in small groups. Tell each other about any such remedies you learned from your parents or grandparents. Then report back to the whole class.

8) Work with a partner, or in small groups. Compile a list of all the things you think should be in a classroom first aid kit. Compare your list with the others. What things does everyone agree on?

Tapescript

UNIT 1 The Telephone Answering Machine

PART A

Presenter: Unit one. The Telephone Answering Machine. Part A.
Female voice: This is the Oxbridge School of English on Oxbridge 876942. We're sorry the school is closed at the moment. Office hours are between nine-thirty a.m. and five-thirty p.m., Monday to Friday. If you have an urgent message please speak after the tone, or you can call us again during office hours. Thank you for your call.

PART B

Presenter: Unit one. The Telephone Answering Machine. Part B.
Irene: Hi! This is Irene. Why are you never at home? I hate speaking to this machine. Anyway, listen. We've got two tickets for the opera for next Saturday night. It's Verdi's *Othello* and Domingo's singing. Rodney can't go because he has to work this weekend. So I wondered if you'd like to come with me instead? It starts at seven. Ring me tomorrow. Oh, but ring before ten because I'm taking Harry to the dentist. Byee!

UNIT 2 'So you wanna keep fit, huh?'

PART A

Presenter: Unit two. So you wanna keep fit, huh? Part A.
Collins: Hi there! I'm Crystal Collins, and I'm very happy to share some time with you. So, you wanna keep fit, huh? Well, you sure came to the right place! Together we can keep fit and healthy, and be more successful. It's easy. Everybody can do it, you hear? Just remember the five golden rules:
Number one. Always wear loose and comfortable clothes when you're exercising. You need to feel comfortable and relaxed.
Number two. You should always do some simple warming-up exercises first. To get your body ready for the real thing.
Number three. Never try to do too much exercise too soon. Take it nice and easy now, you hear? There's no rush about this.
Number four. Don't forget to relax completely for about five minutes when you've finished your workout. You need to rest a little bit after you've been exercising.
And here is golden rule number five. Stop immediately if you feel any pain in your chest, throat, neck or head.

PART B

Presenter: Unit two. So you wanna keep fit, huh? Part B.
Collins: I hope you've done the simple warming-up exercise from the book. You have? Fine! Now I think we're ready for something a little harder. Today's exercise will give you stronger legs and healthier lungs. So put that cigarette out!
You need a strong chair. Stand in front of the chair and put your right foot on the seat. Now step up onto the seat. Stand still. And step back down. Now do it again. This time start with your left foot. On the seat. Step up. Stand still. And step back down. Now. Can you do this ten times? Let's go!

UNIT 3 Inter-City 125

PART A

Presenter: Unit three. Inter-City one two five. Part A.
Guard: May I have your attention please, ladies and gentlemen? This is the guard speaking. Welcome aboard the eleven thirty-five Inter-City service from Edinburgh to London King's Cross calling at Berwick, Newcastle, Durham, Darlington, York, Peterborough and London King's Cross. Passengers for Sunderland change at Newcastle. Passengers for Middlesbrough and Teesside Airport change at Darlington. Passengers for Scarborough change at York. The train is due to arrive at London King's Cross at sixteen forty-five. Thank you.

PART B

Presenter: Unit three. Inter-City one two five. Part B.
Chief Steward: May I have your attention please, ladies and gentlemen? This is the Chief Steward speaking. We would like to inform all passengers that the buffet car is now open. The buffet car is situated towards the middle of the train. On sale are tea, coffee and soft drinks, a selection of fresh and toasted sandwiches including egg and tomato, ham and tomato, egg and cress, roast chicken and toasted cheese; cheeseburgers, beefburgers and sausages and a licensed bar. The buffet car is situated towards the middle of the train. Thank you.

PART C

Presenter: Unit three. Inter-City one two five. Part C.
Chief Steward: Any passengers who require lunch, would you please take your seat in the restaurant car. Would passengers kindly note that there will be only one sitting for lunch, so this is the last and final call for lunch. Any passengers who require lunch, would you please go to the restaurant car now. Thank you.
Guard: Ladies and gentlemen, this is the guard speaking. In a few minutes we will arrive at Berwick. Berwick in a few minutes. Thank you.

UNIT 4 Bibi Khanym and the Origin of the Muslim Veil

Presenter: Unit four. Bibi Khanym and the Origin of the Muslim Veil.
Story-teller: Almost seven centuries ago, in Central Asia, there lived a great king called Tamerlane. He was a mighty, powerful, conquering soldier, and his greatest ambition was that one day he would rule a massive empire stretching from the Atlantic Ocean in the west to the Pacific Ocean in the east. He made his imperial capital in the oasis city of Samarkand, which he planned to make the most beautiful city on earth. Many magnificent mosques were built and they were decorated with exquisite blue ceramic tiles on the outside, and with pure gold on the inside.
Tamerlane, like the great oriental king that he was, had many wives, including a Chinese girl called Bibi Khanym. Now Bibi Khanym was the most beautiful of all Tamerlane's wives, and, as the youngest, she was also the most senior. She was his favourite wife and she was deeply in love with him.
In order to demonstrate her great love of Tamerlane she decided to build a magnificent monument to honour him, while he was away fighting in a distant war. She engaged the best architect, who designed for her the most

magnificent mosque you could imagine. And then she found the best master builder, who began work immediately. But as the weeks and months passed by, the master builder began to fall in love with Bibi Khanym. She resisted all his advances, but at last he threatened to leave the mosque unfinished unless she allowed him to kiss her just once. Bibi Khanym wanted the beautiful mosque finished more than anything else. She was expecting Tamerlane to return any day. So at last she agreed to let the master builder kiss her, just once.
But that was her terrible mistake. For so powerful was the master builder's love for Bibi Khanym that when he kissed her he left a permanent mark on her face.
King Tamerlane returned and saw the guilty mark on his wife's face. The master builder was executed immediately, and then, thinking that a woman's beauty can be a dangerous thing, Tamerlane ordered that from that day and for ever more all the women in the kingdom should never be seen in public without a veil to cover their face.

UNIT 5 Who's who?

PART A

Presenter: Unit five. Who's who? Part A.
Teacher: All right. Hello. I think the best way to start is to get to know each other first. So I'd like each of you to introduce yourself to the rest of us. Just tell us your name . . . and where you're from . . . what you like doing. Just a few words from each person. OK? Who'd like to start? . . . Come on . . . don't be nervous . . . No volunteers?
Göran: OK I'll start.
Teacher: Good. Thank you.
Göran: My name's Göran Sandkvist, and I'm from a little town in Sweden, called Mariestad. I'm a student at the University of Gothenburg . . . er . . . Gothenburg University . . . er . . . do you say Gothenburg University or the University of Gothenburg?
Teacher: Either. Both are correct.
Göran: OK. I'm a student at the University of Gothenburg . . . Er, this summer I travel . . . I have been travelling in England, er, Britain, sorry . . . with two friends. We've been camping and living . . . how do you say . . . living rough?
Teacher: Yes. Living rough. That's a good expression.
Göran: Ja, yes. Er that's why we . . . why I've grown a beard. It was easier not to shave in the mornings when we were camping. . . . Er well . . . that's all . . . I'm just a typical Swede, I think, I like sailing and skiing . . .
Teacher: But you're not blond and tall.
Göran: No. Sorry, I guess you always expect Swedish people to be tall and blond?
Teacher: Perhaps we do. Thank you Göran. Er, how do you spell your name?
Göran: Yes. G – Ö that's O with two dots – R – A – N.
Teacher: OK. Thanks. Now we know a little bit about Göran. Who'd like to introduce themselves next?
Shanti: Er, all right. I will. My name is Shanti. That's S – H – A – N – T – I. And I come from Sri Lanka. Are you still calling it Ceylon?
Teacher: Do we still call it Ceylon? No, we don't. We call your country Sri Lanka, too.
Shanti: All right. I'm from Sri Lanka. Originally. For most of my life I have lived in India. I am also a student, like Göran on my right here, and I have come to Britain to study medicine.
Teacher: Your English is very good, Shanti. Do you speak it at home in India?
Shanti: No, we don't. We speak Tamil. I need to improve my English, especially my listening, because I have to listen to many lectures at the university and it's very difficult for me.
Teacher: All right, Shanti. Thank you. Who's next?
Michel: OK. It's me. I am called Michel. Michel Lavergne. I am from Paris and I . . . er . . . I am . . . er . . . how you say? . . . er . . . a student . . . er . . . a student of er . . .
Teacher: Yes. You're a student?
Michel: Oui, . . . er, I'm sorry, I mean yes.
Teacher: What do you study?
Michel: Yes. What I study? I study er Business Studies. Business Studies. Er . . . I'm married and I have one children . . . er one child. I am very nervous because my English is so bad.
Teacher: No, it's not. Don't worry. Relax.
Michel: I am always nervous. I worry about everything. That's why I lost all my hair.
Teacher: Never mind! My husband's bald, too. Sometimes he wears a badge which says 'Bald Is Beautiful'!
Michel: Yes. We say that grass cannot grow upon a busy street, heh?
Teacher: All right. Thanks very much Michel. Oh, by the way, how do you spell Michel?
Michel: Yes. It's M – I – C – H – E – L.
Teacher: Fine, thanks, now someone else . . .

PART B

Presenter: Unit five. Who's who? Part B.
Policeman: Well, now. We're looking for three people. Two young men and a woman. One of the men is black, the other is white. The woman is also white.
The black man is about twenty-five. He has short, curly black hair. Very short, actually. And a very thin moustache. We understand that he sometimes wears a small, plain gold earring in his right ear and that he often wears dark glasses, er, you know, sunglasses. He was the driver of the car, we think.
Now the second man we're looking for – he's white and about twenty-five to thirty years old. Er, now he's also got curly hair, but it's rather long and it's light brown. Not blond, but not dark, either . . . you know, fair, yes, that's it fair. He has a full moustache but no beard. We think he has a small scar, it's half-moon shaped, on his forehead, just above his left eye . . . er . . . we think his name might be John or Jock or Jack . . . something like that.
And now the third person we're looking for. Well. She's about thirty years old. She's got blonde, wavy, shoulder-length hair. She wears glasses, we think, er rather square, heavy-looking glasses and she sometimes seems to be wearing a silver chain around her neck, with some sort of medallion on it, you know, a St Christopher, or something like that . . .

Tapescript

UNIT 6 Radio Advertisements

PART A

Presenter: Unit six. Radio advertisements. Part A.
Soft male voice: At Simply Sofabeds at Notting Hill Gate we're lowering our prices – for Christmas. Masses of sofabeds for immediate delivery, or choose a fabric from our selection of thousands and we'll deliver your sofa in no time at all. We're open six days a week, with viewing on Sunday. So celebrate Christmas early this year with a Simply Sofabeds sofabed at a price that's right. Simply Sofabeds. One thirty Notting Hill Gate.
Young female voice: Could there really be a women's magazine that's different? Yes. It's called *Prima*. It's packed with news, opinion, fashion and once again there's a free giant pull-out section with clothes to make, crafts to create, beautiful sweaters to knit. Get your second, value-packed issue of *Prima* – (*Prima!*) Only seventy-five pence from your newsagent now.
Male voice: Pianos large, pianos small,
And craftsmen who'll repair them all.
To tune, repair or renovate
Call five three oh, three eight oh eight.
Second male voice: No synthesisers, no hi-tec. Just beautiful pianos at the Wanstead Music Centre. The Wanstead Music Centre. One, High Street, Wanstead.

PART B

Presenter: Unit six. Radio Advertisements. Part B.
Male voice: *Car Buyer* magazine. Every Thursday. It gives you a choice of more new and used cars than all of your local papers put together – and for less. Just thirty pence. *Car Buyer* for car buyers. At your newsagent's now.
Young female voice: Girls! Sensitive skin really does need more sensitive care. And I take special care of my sensitive skin with Cuticura soap. Because Cuticura soap contains a medicated ingredient which cleans your skin without leaving it dry or tight. Cuticura medicated soap. From chemists everywhere.
Bob Harris: Hello. This is Bob Harris inviting you to join me this Friday and every Friday evening for the LBC 'Pop Review'. I play the best of the recent releases, review the British and the American charts, play classic music by the big stars and new tracks by the names of tomorrow. So it's a real mix of different styles and I'm sure you'll love the music. I'd certainly love to have your company. This Friday evening at half-past nine. Right here on LBC.
Jill Lancaster: Er I treated myself to a Servis Quartz and with that came the packet of Ariel automatic.
Young: Since you've been using Ariel, have you ever been tempted to sort of, you know, break away and try something else?
Lancaster: I wouldn't dare. My husband's a police motorcyclist and he has a white shirt every day. Which gives me a lot of dirty collars and cuffs. And I'm a waitress. I have a white shirt every day.
Young: What sort of stains do you tend to get on them?
Lancaster: Erm – it depends what the menu of the day it. It . . . it's usually gravy and er sauces.
Young: Yeah.
Lancaster: And I can pick up the shirts and throw them in the machine with Ariel automatic and the whole job is done. They come out clean and fresh on a low temperature time after time.
Young: Which must be a great relief for you.
Lancaster: It's lovely. (Great.)
Chorus: Swift Interiors – we've got the inside story for you.
Male voice: Let Swift Interiors create that new look for your business. Complete refurbishment from planning through partitioning to air conditioning. Swift Interiors create a look that's right for you.
Chorus: Swift!
Male voice: In the office first impressions count. So contact Swift Interiors for the inside story.
Chorus: Swift Interiors. Call two oh five twenty-one oh seven.
Male voice: Swift Interiors. Two oh five twenty-one oh seven.
Chorus: Swift!

UNIT 7 Terminal One

Presenter: Unit seven. Terminal One.
Announcer 1: British Airways passengers for the British Airways Super Shuttle flight to Edinburgh: this flight is now boarding at gate number four. British Airways Super Shuttle flight to Edinburgh: this flight is now boarding at gate number four.
British Airways passengers wishing to travel to Cork – flight number BA eight three eight – this flight is now checking in at gate number nine. British Airways passengers to Cork on flight number BA eight three eight, this flight is now checking in at gate number nine.
Announcer 2: This is a security announcement. Please do not leave your baggage unattended at any time. And please do not look after baggage left by other people. Please do not leave your baggage unattended at any time. And please do not look after baggage left by other people.
Announcer 3: Would Mr Ian Jackman, recently arrived from Ankara, please go to Airport Information on the ground floor. Mr Ian Jackman recently arrived from Ankara, to Airport Information on the ground floor please.
Announcer 2: Would Dr Raymond Miller from Dublin please contact Airport Information on the ground floor. Dr Raymond Miller from Dublin to Airport Information on the ground floor please.
Announcer 1: Would Mr Simpson, meeting his daughter from Cyprus, please contact Airport Information on the ground floor. Mr Simpson, meeting Yvonne Simpson from Cyprus, please contact Airport Information on the ground floor.
Announcer 2: Aer Lingus passengers to Dublin – flight number AI one four one; this flight is now closing at gate number six. Aer Lingus to Dublin – flight number AI one four one; this flight is now closing at gate number six.
Announcer 4: Would Mrs Waring, meeting a passenger from Larnaca, please contact Airport Information on the ground floor. Mrs Waring meeting a passenger from Larnaca, to Airport Information on the ground floor please.
Announcer 3: Would Captain Jay Brock, from Canada, please contact Airport Information on the ground floor. Captain Jay Brock to Airport Information on the ground floor please.
Announcer 5: British Airways passengers for flight number

BA five six oh to Athens: this flight is now closing at gate number twenty-two.
Would Mr Stephen Sandberg, recently arrived from New York, please contact Airport Information on the ground floor. Mr Stephen Sandberg, recently arrived from New York, to Airport Information on the ground floor please.
Announcer 2: Margaret Murphy, in transit from Düsseldorf to Belfast, please go to Airport Information on the ground floor. Miss Margaret Murphy, in transit from Düsseldorf to Belfast, please contact Airport Information on the ground floor.
This is a security announcement. Please do not leave . . .

UNIT 8 The Touch of Death

Presenter: Unit eight. The Touch of Death.
Narrator: Sally was eighteen. No longer a schoolgirl. No longer a pupil. Next week, she'd be a student. And that was very different.
For eighteen years she'd lived at home. With mum and dad. Sally Anne Roberts, twenty-five Valley Gardens, Richmond, Yorkshire, telephone Richmond five eight oh, three double one. That was who she was. And that was where she lived. But next week? Next week things would be different. She would no longer be living at twenty-five Valley Gardens, Richmond, Yorkshire. She would no longer be living at home. She'd have a new address – and a new home? Her own address anyway. A new place. New friends. New things: furniture, curtains. Not hers, but . . . no, not hers. Someone else bought them. Someone else. Someone she didn't know. Someone she would never meet bought the bed she would sleep in, the cupboard where she'd hang her clothes, the curtains that would cover her windows. Somewhere, down there in that city at the end of the motorway, there was a room. Probably empty right now. At this very minute. Empty. But next week it would have a new owner, and like a once sad puppy it would be bright again. It would be home. Sort of.
She looked around. Her mother had promised to keep her room ready. 'It'll always be here waiting just for you.'
'And my plants? And the goldfish?'
'Oh, yes. Don't you worry my girl', her mother had said with rather too much false happiness in her voice, and none in her eyes. 'I'll water all your plants and I'll feed the goldfish every day.'
That's what she'd said. I'll water all your plants and I'll feed the goldfish every day. And now here she was. A student. In the big city at the end of the motorway. Making her first noisy long distance telephone call home.
Her mother sadly confessed. The plants and goldfish had died already.
Sally hesitated a moment. Then, in a small, small voice, 'How's Dad?' she asked.

UNIT 9 Dial-A-Recipe

PART A

Presenter: Unit nine. Dial-A-Recipe. Chilled Paprika Chicken. Part A.
Female voice: Hello! I'm Valerie, and here's our special telephone recipe for today. It's 'Chilled Paprika Chicken', and it will take no more than an hour to prepare and cook. I hope you've got a pencil and paper ready because I'm going to give you the ingredients. You will need one-and-a-half kilos of cooked chicken – skinned; three hundred millilitres of fresh mayonnaise; one hundred and fifty millilitres of soured cream; one tablespoonful of paprika; two tablespoonfuls of tomato puree; half a teaspoonful of caster sugar; four large tomatoes – skinned and chopped; a little salt, and some freshly ground black pepper.

PART B

Presenter: Unit nine. Dial-A-Recipe. Chilled Paprika Chicken. Part B.
Chris: So that's one kilo of cooked and skinned chicken . . . three hundred millilitres of mayonnaise . . . three hundred millilitres of soured cream . . . a teaspoonful of paprika . . . two tablespoonfuls of tomato puree . . . half a tablespoonful of caster sugar . . . four skinned and chopped tomatoes . . . salt and black pepper.

PART C

Presenter: Unit nine. Dial-A-Recipe. Chilled Paprika Chicken. Part C.
Valerie: To make 'Chilled Paprika Chicken', you should first of all remove all the bones from the chicken. Then, cut the chicken into neat, bite-size cubes. Next, mix the mayonnaise together with the soured cream, the paprika, the tomato puree, sugar, chopped tomatoes and the salt and pepper. All the other ingredients, in fact. Then, when it's thoroughly mixed, add the chicken pieces. Now, stir in the chicken, gently, so that it's completely covered in the sauce. Finally, put your 'Paprika Chicken' into a serving dish or bowl, cover it and put it in the fridge to chill for at least half an hour. 'Chilled Paprika Chicken' is delicious served with a fresh, green salad.

PART D

Presenter: Unit nine. Dial-A-Recipe. Chilled Paprika Chicken. Part D.
Male voice: A green salad is easy to make and it needn't be boring. Take half a lettuce, half a bunch of watercress, a quarter of a cucumber, a green pepper, a few spring onions and about a hundred and twenty millilitres of French dressing.
Core the pepper and take out all the seeds. Then, basically, just chop or slice everything. Put it in a bowl. Pour on the French dressing and toss the salad in the dressing . . . and it's ready to eat.
You can make it much more interesting if you add thinly-sliced hard-boiled eggs, a little fresh lemon juice and lots of nuts and thin slices of avocado pear.
If you do put nuts in your salads put them in just before you eat.

Tapescript

UNIT 10 The Weather Forecast
PART A
Presenter: Unit ten. The Weather Forecast. Part A.
Radio continuity announcer: You're listening to Radio Metro. It's two minutes to nine, and time for the latest weather forecast from Dan Francis at the London Weather Centre.
Francis: Hello. It's been another warm and fine day for most of us. Temperatures in south-east England reached twenty-six degrees Celsius by mid-afternoon, and Brighton had fifteen hours of lovely sunshine. Further north it was a little cooler with maximum temperatures of around twenty-one degrees in southern Scotland, and in the far north-west of Scotland there were some light showers around midday. But the rest of the country, as I said, has been warm and dry with temperatures in the Midlands reaching twenty-three degrees Celsius by early afternoon although it was a little cooler along the west coast and in Northern Ireland.
But already the weather's beginning to change, I'm afraid, and during the night showers will slowly move in from the Atlantic to reach south-west England and southern coasts of Wales by early morning.
The rest of the country will have a very mild, dry night with minimum temperatures no lower than fifteen degrees in the south, a little cooler – eleven degrees or so – in the north. Any remaining showers in northwest Scotland will pass quickly to leave a mild, dry night there too.
And now the outlook for Friday and the weekend. Well, southern Europe will, once . . .

PART B
Presenter: Unit ten. The Weather Forecast. Part B.
Francis: Well, southern Europe will, once again, get the best of the weekend weather, and if your holiday starts this weekend then southern Spain is the place to be, with temperatures of thirty-four degrees along the Mediterranean coast. At the eastern end of the Med, too, you can expect uninterrupted sunshine and temperatures of up to thirty-two degrees Celsius in Greece and south-east Italy, but further north the weather's not so settled. Much of France, Belgium and the Netherlands will be cloudy with occasional rain and maximum temperatures will be around twenty-two degrees – very disappointing for this time of year.
Scotland and Northern Ireland will have heavy rain for much of the weekend and temperatures will drop to a cool seventeen degrees. Across most of England the weather will be cloudy but mainly dry with sunny periods. And when the sun does come out temperatures could rise to a maximum of twenty-three degrees.

UNIT 11 Buying a New Car
PART A
Presenter: Unit eleven. Buying a New Car. Part A.
Monica: All right. Where do we start?
George: I think we should draw up a list of advantages and disadvantages for each car, don't you?
Monica: Yes, OK. Er . . . OK. Let's start with the Renault 5. Why did you like that? I thought it was rather expensive, actually.
George: Well. It's six thousand six hundred and seventy-five pounds. That's for the TSE model, with a five-speed gearbox.
Monica: That's more than we can really afford you know, George.
George: Yes. I suppose it is. But it has got a fourteen hundred cc engine –
Monica: The same as the Ford Escort.
George: Yes and a hundred ccs bigger than the MG Metro.
Monica: Yeah, but the MG is a lot cheaper. It's . . . six two nine nine, call it six thousand three hundred. It's almost four hundred pounds cheaper.
George: All right. Let's look at the MG, then.
It's got a thirteen hundred cc engine, costs six thousand two hundred and ninety-nine pounds . . . what about petrol? Have you got the mpg figures?
Monica: Er . . . yes . . . er . . . according to this . . . the MG does fifty-six miles per gallon. That's very good, don't you think?
George: Yes, but the Renault does exactly the same, and that's got a bigger engine, remember.
Monica: Actually, they're all about the same on petrol. Look, the Escort does fifty-seven. How much does it cost?
George: Escort, Escort . . . well, . . . the GL – that's the fourteen hundred cc one – er . . . that costs seven thousand one hundred and eighty-two pounds . . .
Monica: George. We simply can't afford to go over six thousand five hundred pounds.
George: I know. I think that means we can forget the Volkswagen Golf, too, don't you?
Monica: How much is it?
George: Eight thousand and ninety. That's for the GL model with a sixteen hundred cc engine. And it only does forty-seven miles per gallon. Yeah. It's too big and we can't afford it.
Monica: OK. So what about the Peugeot two oh five, then?
George: Well. The three-door XS model costs six thousand two hundred and twenty-five pounds. It's got a fourteen hundred cc engine.
Monica: How about petrol?
George: It does fifty-four mpg, according to this. I think it looks great.
Monica: I know you do. You like it because it looks more like a sports car than the others.
George: It also looks the most modern, don't you think?
Monica: Have they all got three doors?
George: The MG has three. The Golf has five, but we can forget about the Golf. The Escort has five and the Renault . . . that's got three.
Monica: Do you really think the MG's as reliable as the others?
George: Probably not. I don't know . . . but probably not.
Monica: So that leaves the Escort, the Renault and the Peugeot two oh five . . .
George: You like French cars, don't you?
Monica: Don't you?
George: Not really.
Monica: But I thought the Peugeot was your favourite.
George: Well. If the Escort's too expensive . . .
Monica: And a little bit boring.
George: And a little bit boring. That just leaves us with . . .

PART B

Presenter: Unit eleven. Buying a New Car. Part B.
Radio presenter: ... and the car we tested was the GT. It's the most expensive model in the range and at eleven thousand eight hundred and sixty-nine pounds it is, I think, a little overpriced: you can buy the equivalent Volkswagen for almost eight hundred pounds less. But it's a beautiful car and I'd been looking forward to driving it for a long time. Unfortunately, I had problems right from the start. The day I tested the car was one of the few sunny days we had this summer. So, naturally enough, I decided to open the sun-roof. But the handle was so stiff that it was almost impossible to move it. I did, eventually, get the sun-roof open but as it finally began to slide back it made the most awful noise. Noise, I'm afraid, is quite a feature of this car. The car's interior seemed to be very badly insulated against engine noise, and with the sun-roof finally open the noise of the wind was very loud indeed.
In general, the car was quite comfortable, but I didn't really have enough leg room, and I found it difficult to adjust the wing mirrors to the position I wanted.
The test car was, of course, brand new, but I did find quite a lot of small scratches and badly finished paintwork around the headlights and radiator grille. And the silver plastic strip which runs along each side of the car wasn't properly fixed to the car body on the left hand side of the car I tested.
So, quite a lot of irritating faults in a car you're going to have to pay ...

UNIT 12 The London Marathon

Presenter: Unit twelve. The London Marathon.
Rob Jackson: I was very nervous at the start. The red start is for people who've never run in a marathon before. There were about ten thousand of us. It wasn't really possible to run for the first mile or so; there were just too many people, so we just jogged very gently down Charlton Road.
I was jogging quite nicely, you know, nice and gently, by the time I reached that left turn into John Wilson Street, but everyone seemed to be running faster than me ... that's where the elite runners join with everyone else. The elite are those people who have run in official marathons before. I'm sure I saw Greta Waitz pass me as we turned left into Woolwich Church Street. She's the Norwegian runner who won the Women's Marathon in 1983.
I was surprised to see the Cutty Sark so quickly. It's more than ten kilometres from the start. There were hundreds of people all along Woolwich Road and Romney Road – and then you turn sharp right, round the Cutty Sark, back into Creek Street and up Evelyn Road. That's when Ingrid Kristiansen passed me. She's another Norwegian woman who won in eighty-four and eighty-five.
At Surrey Docks we turned right into Redriff Road and then the route follows the river along Rotherhithe Street. I was starting to feel a bit tired and worried ... then I realised I was in Jamaica Road – and Tower Bridge is just at the top of Jamaica Road. People were dancing in the street, there was music and everyone was cheering us and shouting encouragement ...
Once I'd crossed the bridge and was running along Cable Street I felt much better because I knew I'd completed more than half the race – about twenty-four kilometres in fact. We ran along East India Dock Road and turned south into the Isle of Dogs. It was very quiet round there, and I think that was the first time I seriously thought I wouldn't finish the race. Westferry Road seemed endless and my legs were getting very heavy. I started to think about some of the people who'd won the marathon in previous years: Inge Simonsen from Norway and Dick Beardsley the American; they won it together in nineteen eighty-one. Then all those British runners: Joyce Smith in eighty-one and eighty-two; Hugh Jones, Mike Gratton, Charlie Spedding and Steve Jones. Thinking about something always helps you when you're running.
I suddenly realised that I was in The Highway. The route turns left, through St Katharine's Dock and then you can see Tower Bridge for the second time.
This time you go under the bridge. Then along Lower Thames Street, past the Monument, through the underpass at Blackfriars and into Victoria Embankment.
And that's where I began to feel really tired. You've done about forty kilometres, and you just want to stop. My legs were like wood, but I managed to keep going. The crowds were fantastic. They help you enormously. You turn right, up Northumberland Avenue and then at Admiralty Arch you just go straight down The Mall with Buckingham Palace in front of you. Left at the top, into Birdcage Walk. It's a fantastic feeling because as you run down Birdcage Walk the pain in your legs and the noise in your head is almost unbearable. But you can see Westminster Bridge and then Big Ben and you begin to realise that you – *you* – have actually completed the London Marathon.

UNIT 13 The People's Republic of China: Facts and Figures

PART A

Presenter: Unit thirteen. The People's Republic of China: Facts and Figures. Part A.
Radio presenter: China! It's the world's oldest surviving civilisation. It has an uninterrupted history going back over four thousand years. After the Soviet Union and Canada it is the third largest country in the world and more people live here than anywhere else on Earth; one billion of them – a quarter of the world's population. So, one person in every four in the world is Chinese!
The People's Republic of China shares borders with twelve states. Starting in the north-east, they are North Korea, the Soviet Union, Mongolia, Afghanistan, Pakistan, India, Nepal, Sikkim, Bhutan, Burma, Laos and Vietnam.

PART B

Presenter: Unit thirteen. The People's Republic of China: Facts and Figures. Part B.
Radio Presenter: ... Burma, Laos and Vietnam.
Now, many of the things we use in our everyday lives were invented and developed in ancient China. Did you know, for example, that the Chinese gave the world paper and printing, money, and fireworks, and silk; they even invented sunglasses.
Although it is now a major world power, we know less about China today – modern China – than about almost any other country. This series of programmes will look at what life is like in China today.
Let's start then with a few basic facts and figures about the land and population. The total area of the People's Republic of China is about nine million, five hundred and seventy-

Tapescript

five thousand square kilometres. The size of the population is around one thousand million – a billion people. Although seventy-nine percent of the population live in the countryside and only twenty-one percent live in the cities, China has more than twelve cities with more than two million inhabitants. The biggest cities in China are Shanghai, which has around twelve million inhabitants, Beijing the capital, with a total of some nine-and-a-half million, Tianjin with eight million, and Chongqing with six million, six hundred thousand inhabitants.

UNIT 14 A Valuable Collection?

PART A

Presenter: Unit fourteen. A Valuable Collection? Part A.
Journalist: Er ... roughly, when did you begin collecting badges?
Simpson: At my primary school, I think. The teachers used to give out badges to pupils who were particularly good at certain things. So I got a little blue badge with the word 'swimming' on it, and then another one I remember – it was green – which had the word 'Tidy' on it! Ha!
Journalist: And have you still got those badges in your collection?
Simpson: No ... well, I've got the swimming badge, but I think I was so untidy that I must have lost the tidy badge years ago!
Journalist: And you started collecting badges, then, from what, the age of about nine?
Simpson: Er, yeah, I guess so ... eight or nine or so. That's right. In those days – we're talking about the early fifties – there weren't so many cars around as there are today. So filling stations didn't have so many customers. So the petrol companies used to give out badges. I suppose they thought that kids whose parents had a car would keep asking them to go to a particular filling station so that they could get another free badge. My dad bought our first car in nineteen fifty-six I think it was – a black Ford Popular – and every time I went out with him in it I used to ask him to go to a different petrol station so that I could add more to my growing badge collection.
Actually, he was a very shy man, my father, and I'm sure he didn't like asking for free things ...
Journalist: So petrol company badges were the first ones in your collection were they?
Simpson: After 'swimming' and 'tidy', yeah ... But soon all sorts of companies started making badges to advertise their products, even cigarette companies. I've got one in my collection for Wills's Woodbines – they were the cheapest cigarettes in those days – and on the badge, at the bottom, it says, 'Smoked by Millions' – no health warnings in those days ...

PART B

Presenter: Unit fourteen. A Valuable Collection? Part B.
Journalist: How did you start collecting foreign badges?
Simpson: I started travelling! Actually, I have to say that as a teenager I rather lost interest in badges and in fact I threw away a lot ... or, er lost quite a lot ... ones which would be rather valuable today. But when I left University I got a job in Austria and whenever I had a holiday, I used to take cheap trips to countries in Eastern Europe. Badges are very popular there and I soon started collecting again. I've got some really beautiful badges from Czechoslovakia and the Soviet Union, and some lovely ones from Yugoslavia, too.
Journalist: Do people in Eastern Europe wear badges or do they just collect them?
Simpson: Oh no, they wear them just like we do.
Journalist: Why do you think people do wear badges?
Simpson: Well, I think there are probably three main reasons. I think some people wear them to show that they belong to something. You know, like a group or a club or an association of some sort ... like the Rotary Club or a trade union.
And then I think people wear badges because they have something to say to the world. To tell people what they think – political or religious badges – which show what kind of person the wearer is, what he or she believes in, what they want to communicate ... or badges which say things like, er, 'Please don't smoke near me' or 'I'm a vegetarian'. I think that sort of badge is very popular these days.
Journalist: You said you thought there were three main reasons why people wear badges ...
Simpson: Oh, yes. Well, the third reason, I think, is to show everyone else where you've been ... you know, badges which say things like 'I've been to Disneyland'. A lot of people put stickers like that on their cars, too.
There are other reasons, of course, but I think they're the main ones.

PART C

Presenter: Unit fourteen. A Valuable Collection? Part C.
Journalist: There are quite a lot of political badges in your collection aren't there?
Simpson: Yes. I've got a lot of anti-nuclear badges. The anti-nuclear groups do seem to use badges quite a lot.
Journalist: And humorous ones?
Simpson: The funny ones? No, not really. I've got a few but I don't really like them so much. I prefer badges which have some kind of social history about them ...
Journalist: So which are your favourite badges then?
Simpson: Oh! That's impossible to say. I like the British badges I've got from the nineteen fifties, because they were the ones I used to wear, as a kid, I mean ... they mean the most to me ... but then these badges from Central Africa ... they were so difficult to get and they remind me very much of the hard time I had travelling and working there ...
Journalist: Are they valuable? Is yours a valuable collection?
Simpson: They're valuable to me. I mean, you could never replace them. But I'm not sure they're worth a lot of money. I don't think I'd get much for them if I ever tried to sell them ...

UNIT 15 What's in a Name?

PART A

Presenter: Unit fifteen. What's in a Name? Part A.
Lecturer: What do you think is the most important thing about a car? The engine? No. The design? Nope! Its reliability? Uh-uh! What then? Well, would it surprise you to discover that the most important thing about a car is its name. It's true. The Volkswagen Golf is called a Rabbit in the United States. The Ford Scorpio is called the Granada in Great Britain. When Rolls-Royce were developing the Silver Shadow, in the nineteen sixties, they wanted to call it the Silver Mist. Beautiful, huh? The Rolls-Royce Silver Mist. Then someone made a very important discovery. They

discovered that the word *mist*, in German, means garbage, rubbish, junk, . . . You see, William Shakespeare was wrong. Can you imagine some big shot movie star riding around in his new Rolls-Royce Silver Junk!?

The nineteen sixties were a time of relative prosperity. People had more money than ever before. Some people were aggressively successful, and this was reflected in the names of the fast and powerful sports cars of that time: Stingray, Spitfire, Tiger, Avenger.

And then psychologists began to study driving and drivers. They found that people who drove cars which had very aggressive names had more road accidents than people who drove cars with less aggressive names.

So, in the nineteen seventies we had the Reliant Kitten, the Austin Maxi, the Triumph Herald, the Opel Kadett. Simple, plain, ordinary, Mr Nice-Guy names.

But, you know, to most people, their car is much more than private transport, and not everyone wants to drive a car called a Kitten. People like to fantasise a little. When you're sitting behind the wheel of an automobile anything is possible. You are liberated. You have the freedom to go where you want, when you want. The open road is ahead. It's romantic. And look at the romantic names the manufacturers give their cars today: Sierra, Scirocco, Montego, Savanna, Fuego.

And today's big, powerful and expensive cars have big, powerful and expensive names. Names like Corniche, Camargue and Mulsanne.

Most of us, of course, cannot possibly ever hope to afford such status symbols. But the car manufacturers keep us happy with our little city cars. They give them happy names. Names like Mini, Uno, Polo and Charade. And it's still possible to have romantic fantasies even if you can only afford a Fiesta or a Samba.

For the serious driver there are serious cars. And these don't have names. They have numbers. A car with a number seems more reliable, more technically advanced, safer, like an airliner. So there's the Volvo 760, the BMW 745i, the Jaguar XJ6, the Mercedes-Benz 190, the Audi 100, the Rover 800 . . .

PART **B**

Presenter: Unit fifteen. What's in a Name? Part B.
Narrator: 'This morning His Highness took me out for a drive in one of his cars. He knows no more about cars than I do and chooses them by the appeal of their names. So he bought a 'Sunbeam'. It would surely be a very pretty car; but it seemed much the same as any other, and he was equally disappointed by a 'Moon'. He asked me today what his next car should be, for two of the four he already has are getting very old, and I suggested a 'Buick', which was the only make I could call to mind; but after pronouncing the word two or three times with evident disfavour, and making it sound like a sneeze, he did not refer to the matter again.'

UNIT 16 'Value For Money'

Presenter: Unit sixteen. Value For Money.
Male radio presenter: (Martin Hart) Hello. And welcome to this week's 'Value For Money'. Now, Jan, you've been looking at coffee machines for us this week, is that right? Surely, they're all more or less the same, aren't they?
Female radio presenter: (Janet Hill) Hello, Martin. Well, that's just what I thought, too. You just pour in the water, spoon in the coffee, switch on the machine and wait. Well, not exactly. We tested five machines: the Kaffematic 25, er . . . made in West Germany; the Coffee Master de-luxe, made in the U.K.; the Domestika Electric Coffee Pot, from Czechoslovakia; the Aromacup Two Thousand – another one from Britain, that one; and finally the Kaffitalia Automatic, which, as its name suggests, is made in Italy.
Martin: And what did we find?
Janet: Well. The first thing we looked at was the price. And we found a difference of ten pounds between the cheapest and the most expensive.
Martin: So how much is the Kaffematic?
Janet: That's the most expensive, er . . . it's twenty-nine pounds ninety-five.
Martin: And the cheapest?
Janet: The Domestika. That was only nineteen pounds ninety-five.
Martin: So why doesn't everyone buy a Domestika, then?
Janet: Well. It's not as simple as that. They don't all make the same amount of coffee – but let me give you the prices of the others, first. The Coffee Master is twenty-five pounds seventy-five; the Aromacup is twenty-two fifty, and the Kaffitalia costs twenty-six ninety-five.
Martin: You said they don't all make the same amount of coffee.
Janet: That's right. You get twelve cups of coffee from the Kaffematic, but only eight from both the Coffee Master and the Domestika. The Kaffitalia gives you about nine cups and you get ten cups out of the Aromacup.
Martin: So how can you decide which machine is the best value for money?
Janet: Well, Martin, you look at all the extras.
Martin: Extras?
Janet: That's right. You see, with the Kaffematic you get one kilo of coffee and one packet of filter papers absolutely free. And the machine has a plug.
Martin: That's . . . that sounds good.
Janet: Yes. None of the other machines has a plug when you buy it.
Martin: The Kaffematic's the only one.
Janet: Yes. You have to buy a plug separately for all the other machines.
Martin: Do you get free coffee with all of them?
Janet: Not at all. As I said, you get one kilo with the Kaffematic, but you get none at all with the Coffee Master, the Domestika or the Kaffitalia. And with the Aromacup you only get a half-kilo packet.
Martin: And what about filter papers?
Janet: Well, there it's a little better. You get a packet of filter paper free with every machine we tested, except the Domestika.
Martin: I suppose filter papers are cheaper to give away free than coffee.
Janet: I suppose so.
Martin: What about guarantees?
Janet: Each one comes with a twelve month guarantee.
Martin: Jan, it's really very difficult to know which is the best value for money.
Janet: It is, Martin. I agree. We found that both the Aromacup and the Kaffematic were not very good at keeping the coffee hot. I poured myself a cup from the Aromacup and it was really too cold to enjoy. The Kaffematic's coffee was a little warmer, but it wasn't really

Tapescript

hot. The hottest coffee came from the Domestika.
Martin: How reliable do you think the Domestika is? I mean, in this country we sometimes think that electrical goods from Eastern Europe are not very good, don't we? Not very safe, perhaps.
Janet: I don't know, Martin. But if you need spare parts to repair it, they'll be very difficult to find, I should think . . .

UNIT 17 Programming the Video

PART A

Presenter: Unit seventeen. Programming the Video. Part A.
Shop Assistant: . . . OK, now this is the instruction booklet. Er, it tells you everything you need to know about how to operate the machine . . .
Charlotte: Yes. Fine. Thank you. But I wonder if you could just go through it . . . I mean can you just show me how to record a programme? . . . I'm one of those people who . . . well, I understand things much better when someone actually shows me what to do . . . what buttons I have to press, and so on . . . you know . . .
Assistant: Yes, of course. Well. All the buttons are here, behind this panel, this little plastic door. So you have to open the panel and the first thing you have to do is check two things. Er . . . first, you have to ask 'Is the machine switched on?' You press the OPERATE switch to switch it on.
The second thing is, is there a tape in it? Here's a tape . . . er, actually, I'll give you this one with the machine, they're . . .
Charlotte: Thanks. Are they expensive, these tapes?
Assistant: Er, not really, no. You can get a very good four-hour tape for less than ten pounds. Now. Put the tape in here.
OK. Now you're ready. The machine's switched on and there's a tape inside. Now, when the TV programme starts you just press these two buttons, first the RECORD button and then the PLAY button. And when the programme's finished, just press this one, the STOP button.
Charlotte: Fine. Now what about programming the machine, you know, to er, to record a programme while I'm out?

PART B

Presenter: Unit seventeen. Programming the Video. Part B.
Charlotte: . . . you know, to er, to record a programme while I'm out?
Assistant: Yes. Of course. Well, if you want to record a programme while you're out, you have to programme the machine.
Charlotte: All right. How do I do that? Is it difficult, complicated, I mean?
Assistant: Not at all. It's really very simple and straightforward. First, you have to make sure the machine is switched on.
Charlotte: The OPERATE switch.
Assistant: The OPERATE switch. And also don't forget to put a tape in. Then you press the PROGRAMME button.
Charlotte: The PROGRAMME button?
Assistant: Yes. This one here. Now these little numbers which are flashing – they're the machine's memory positions. You see you can programme this machine to record four things over two weeks. Now we want number one, because this is the first thing we're going to programme. So you have to press the SET button once.
Then you have to press the STORE button. That keeps it in the machine's memory.
Charlotte: It stores it.
Assistant: Yeah. Now you can see the channel numbers are flashing. Let's say that the programme we want to record is going to be on Channel 4. You have to press the SET button again, four times. Two . . . three . . . four. That's it. Now press STORE again, so that it's in the memory.
Charlotte: Now the clock's flashing.
Assistant: That's right. Now we have to programme the day and time. Let's say the programme we want is on Wednesday. You have to press the SET button again until you see 'Wednesday' in the display. There. Monday, Tuesday, Wednesday. Now press STORE again and it's in the memory . . .

PART C

Presenter: Unit seventeen. Programming the Video. Part C.
Assistant: So, we've got the channel . . . Channel 4 . . . and the day . . . Wednesday . . . Now you see the clock's still flashing so we can programme the start and finish times. You have to press and hold the SET button until the clock shows the time you want. Let's say your programme starts at eight o'clock.
. . . six . . . seven . . . eight. That's it. Don't forget to press the STORE button again.
Charlotte: OK. And if the programme finishes at, say, nine o'clock?
Assistant: Then you have to press the SET button again until you see nine o'clock on the clock. Then press STORE once more. So that's just about it, really. Simple enough. The machine is programmed to record on Channel 4, on Wednesday, from eight till nine.
Charlotte: It's quite straightforward really, isn't it? I mean you just have to press SET and STORE, basically.
Assistant: More or less, yeah.
Charlotte: And if you make a mistake? I mean what happens if I set the machine to record at eight o'clock, but I really wanted seven o'clock? How do I change it if I've already pressed STORE?
Assistant: Just press this button.
Charlotte: RESET?
Assistant: Yes. And then just start programming from the beginning again.

UNIT 18 The Department Store

Presenter: Unit eighteen. The Department Store.
Store Announcer: Welcome to Spring-time at Bentley's. It's Italian Week in our Food Halls, on the Ground Floor. Try our delicious pasta. It's made fresh every day. Or Bentley's specially imported Parmesan cheese. And don't forget the wine. All this week Italian Lambrusco is only two pounds fifty a bottle. So celebrate Spring Italian style in Bentley's Food Halls, on the Ground Floor.
And now that the good weather's finally arrived, there's plenty of work to do in the garden. And to help you get started we're reducing the cost of garden tools. There's five pounds off Wilkinson garden forks and three pounds fifty off spades and rakes. And, if you spend fifteen pounds or more we'll give you a pair of gardening gloves absolutely free. So hurry on down to the Gardening Department in the Basement.
Looking for something cool? The Spring collection has just

arrived in the Ritz Boutique on the Second Floor. Hundred per cent cotton sweaters from twelve pounds ninety-nine, skirts from fourteen pounds. And why not take a closer look at the exciting range of *Yankie Girl* cosmetics? It's not too early to think of summer. We have the very latest swimwear from France and exciting beachwear at unbelievable prices – all in the Ritz Boutique on the Second Floor.

Feeling tired? Ready for a mid-morning break? Pop into Bentley's Coffee Shop on the Third Floor and choose from four blends of freshly ground coffee or five different varieties of Indian and Chinese tea. There are cold drinks, too, and a tasty selection of biscuits, cakes and sandwiches. But if you want more than just a snack, our restaurant is open for lunch every day from twelve till three. That's our Coffee Shop on the Third Floor and our air-conditioned restaurant on the Fourth Floor.

And finally, just a word or two about our new Sports Department. It's moved. And it's grown. Now on the First Floor, our Sports Department is bigger than ever. There's the full range of Dunlop training shoes starting at nine ninety-five, a wide variety of track suits from sixteen pounds and an impressive range of tennis rackets from nine pounds fifty to ninety-five pounds. Our specially-trained staff can help you choose the clothes and equipment that are right for you.

Bentley's accept all the major credit cards, and, of course, we have our own credit scheme. If you want to know more about opening an account, ask for a leaflet in any department, or visit the Customer Services Department on the Ground Floor.

We're here to help you. It's Spring all the year round at Bentley's. Happy shopping!

UNIT 19 Radio Phone-In

PART A

Presenter: Unit nineteen. Radio Phone-In. Part A.
Radio presenter: Good afternoon. And welcome to our midweek phone-in. In today's programme we're going to concentrate on personal problems. And here with me in the studio I've got Tessa Colbeck, who writes the agony column in *Flash* magazine, and Doctor Maurice Rex, Student Medical Adviser at the University of Norfolk.
The number to ring with your problem is oh one, if you're outside London, two two two, two one two two. And we have our first caller on the line, and it's Rosemary, I think, er calling from Manchester. Hello Rosemary.
Rosemary: Hello.
Radio presenter: How can we help you, Rosemary?
Rosemary: Well, it's my dad. He won't let me stay out after ten o'clock at night and all my friends can stay out much longer than that. I always have to go home first. It's really embarrassing . . .
Tessa: Hello, Rosemary, love. Rosemary, how old are you dear?
Rosemary: I'm fifteen in two months' time.
Tessa: And where do you go at night – when you go out?
Rosemary: Just to my friend's house, usually. But everyone else can stay there much later than me. I have to leave at about quarter to ten.
Tessa: And does this friend of yours . . . does she live near you?
Rosemary: It takes about ten minutes to walk from her house to ours.
Tessa: I see. You live in Brighton, was it? Well, Brighton's . . .
Rosemary: No. Manchester . . . I live in Manchester.
Tessa: Oh. I'm sorry, love. I'm getting mixed up. Yes, well Manchester's quite a rough city isn't it? I mean, your dad . . .
Rosemary: No. Not really. Not where we live it isn't. I don't live in the City Centre or anything like that. And Christine's house is in a very quiet part.
Tessa: Christine. That's your friend, is it?
Rosemary: Yeah. That's right. I mean, I know my dad gets worried but it's perfectly safe.
Maurice: Rosemary. Have you talked about this with your dad?
Rosemary: No. He just shouts and then he says he won't let me go out at all if I can't come home on time.
Maurice: Why don't you just try to sit down quietly with your dad – sometime when he's relaxed – and just have a quiet chat about it? He'll probably explain why he worries about you. It isn't always safe for young girls to go out at night.
Tessa: Yes. And maybe you could persuade him to come and pick you up from Christine's house once or twice.
Rosemary: Yes. I don't think he'll agree to that, but I'll talk to him about it. Thanks.

PART B

Presenter: Unit nineteen. Radio Phone-In. Part B.
Radio presenter: All right. Thank you for that call, Rosemary. We now go, I think, to Glasgow and our next caller, er, Jim Baillie. Hello Jim.
Jim: Hello?
Radio presenter: Hello Jim. What's your problem?
Jim: Er . . . well I'm er . . . beginning to lose my hair. Er, I went to the doctor, but he just said there was nothing I can do about it. He said it was probably hereditary. My father was bald by the time he was thirty.
Maurice: Hello, Jim. And how old are you?
Jim: Me. I'm twenty-eight.
Maurice: And are you losing a lot of hair, then?
Jim: Well, it comes out a lot when I comb my hair and you can see a thin part on the top of my head.
Maurice: And does that really worry you, Jim?
Jim: Well. I don't like it. It's old . . . you know . . . looks old . . . I don't want to look like a middle-aged man at twenty-eight. And I wondered if there was some special shampoo I should use . . . if you could tell me one that I should buy . . . something like that . . . you know . . . to stop it getting worse.
Maurice: Well, you know, Jim, to be honest with you there's not really a lot you can do about it, actually, I'm afraid. I mean, baldness is one of those things that, in my experience, you just have to try to accept. Some men find it more difficult to accept baldness than others . . .
Tessa: There is one piece of advice, though, Jim, and that's don't try to comb your hair over the bald or thin patch. Don't try to hide it. Whatever you do, don't comb it over because that usually looks ridiculous. And the other thing that usually looks ridiculous is a man with a wig. Don't let anyone persuade you to buy one of those false hairpiece things, because they usually look much worse than a bald man. I actually think bald men can look very attractive. My husband's bald and I think it really suits him.

Tapescript

PART C
Presenter: Unit nineteen. Radio Phone-In. Part C.
Radio presenter: And I think we've just about got time for one more quick call. And we've got Martin on the line. Martin, you're calling from London, is that right?
Martin: That's right, Mary.
Radio presenter: Fine. Now, what's your problem, Martin?
Martin: I've been trying to stop smoking for a long time and I'm finding it very difficult. I wondered if Tessa or Maurice had any useful tips.
Tessa: How long have you been trying to stop smoking, Martin?
Martin: About three years.
Tessa: Three years! Good heavens! Quite a long time, then . . .
Martin: Yes. You see, the problem is I work in an office where I'm the only smoker, and my girlfriend doesn't smoke . . .
Tessa: So why do you think you can't stop, Martin?
Martin: Well, I don't know. Maybe I'm just not trying hard enough, you see . . .
Maurice: Martin. When you stopped smoking before, in the past, what was the longest amount of time you stopped for?
Martin: About six months.
Maurice: And why did you start again, do you think?
Martin: Well, my job is very demanding. You know. I have to work quite late at the office. Quite a lot, actually. And I find that cigarettes help me . . . you know . . . when I'm stressed . . . under pressure . . .
Maurice: Martin. If I were you, I think I'd start to try to . . .

UNIT 20 First Aid

Presenter: Unit twenty. First Aid.
Medical voice: As any parent will tell you, small cuts and minor grazes are unavoidable among small children. Such cuts and grazes will usually need little or no treatment. The bleeding will clean the wound naturally, and it should stop within a few minutes, as the blood clots and dries. More serious cuts may need to be gently cleaned with soft cotton and warm water. They should then be dressed with a clean cotton bandage.
Follow this simple checklist of questions. Ask yourself each of these questions in order to make sure you treat cuts and grazes properly:
First. Is the cut on the face? If it is, call a doctor as soon as possible – especially if the eye is injured.
Second. Is the cut bleeding badly? If it is, put a clean piece of cotton wool over it and press down firmly for about five minutes.
Thirdly. Ask yourself if the cut is still bleeding badly. If it is, dress it with a clean cotton bandage and call a doctor as soon as possible.
Fourthly. Is the cut a deep one, and is it wide open? If it is, clean the cut gently, with clean cotton wool and a little warm water, then hold it closed with an adhesive dressing.
Fifth question. Was the cut made by a nail or a long, sharp piece of wood? If it was, there may be some dirt in the cut. Let it bleed for a while, to clean itself. Then clean it with cotton wool and warm water and dress it with a clean cotton bandage.
Finally, don't forget that young children can become very easily upset or shocked by a cut – especially if it is a serious one. Try to keep them calm, and quiet. Don't give them anything to drink, but keep their lips wet with a little water.

Answer key

UNIT 1 The Telephone Answering Machine

1 c
2 Oxbridge 876942
3 a) No   c) Yes
  b) Yes   d) No
4 b and c
5 c
6 a) True   e) False
  b) False f) True
  c) False g) True
  d) True   h) False
7 c
9 Rodney is probably Irene's husband and Harry is probably their son *or* Rodney could be Irene's boyfriend or boss and Harry could be her brother.

UNIT 2 'So you wanna keep fit, huh?'

1 b, e, f, h and j
2 a) forehead   b) cheek   c) chin   d) throat
  e) chest   f) armpit   g) lungs   h) elbow
  i) stomach   j) wrist   k) knuckles   l) legs
  m) ankle   n) feet
3 g – lungs, l – legs, n – feet
5 a) ... feet apart.
  b) ... arm (above your head).
  c) ... your head.
  d) ... this, with your left arm.
  e) ... both arms (together).

UNIT 3 Inter-City 125

1 11.35
2 16.45
3 Edinburgh, Berwick, Newcastle, Durham, Darlington, York, Peterborough, London
  a) Newcastle
  b) Darlington
  c) York
4 **Drinks:** tea, cola/lemonade, beer, wines, spirits, coffee
  Sandwiches: egg and tomato, ham and tomato, roast chicken
  Hot food: cheeseburgers, sausage (but no chips)
5 Some suggestions:
  a) Restaurant cars have a waiter/waitress service.
  b) You sit down at a table to eat a meal in the restaurant car.
  c) The restaurant car is probably more expensive.
  d) The food may be better in the restaurant car. It may be fast food or 'junk' food in the buffet.
  e) You probably don't have to queue in the restaurant car.
  f) The restaurant car usually has fixed times for meals.
  g) In the buffet car you can buy single items. In the restaurant car you probably have to have a complete meal.
6 The sign shows a personal stereo and should appeal to anyone whose journey has been spoiled by the high-pitched, tinny sound which you can sometimes hear when other passengers are listening to music through such a machine. Perhaps the sign should appear in **confined** public places. (**Note**: it is already in use on the London Underground).

UNIT 4 Bibi Khanym and the Origin of the Muslim Veil

1 ... (a) dangerous (thing).
2

> 7th century – Central Africa – powerful soldier – great empire – Atlantic to Indian Ocean – capital mountain city Samarkand – many mosques – blue ceramic tiles <u>inside</u> – gold outside.
>
> T. had many wives – favourite <u>Arab</u> girl – B.K. – most beautiful – <u>oldest</u> most important wife.
>
> B.K. decided build mosque – found architect – work started immediate<u>ly</u>
>
> B.K. fell in love with master builder – mosque finished – T. returns home – killed B.K. and builder – Muslim women wear veil <u>in</u> memo<u>ry</u> of B.K.

3 a) True   d) True   g) True   j) False
  b) True   e) False   h) False
  c) True   f) False   i) False

UNIT 5 Who's who?

1 a) Göran, Sweden (4)
  b) Shanti, Sri Lanka (5)
  c) Michel, France (7)
2 a) True   f) True
  b) False   g) False
  c) False   h) True
  d) True   i) False
  e) True   j) False
3 a)  b) c)

UNIT 6 Radio Advertisements

1 a) Simply Sofabeds   b) furniture
     Prima women's magazine   magazine
     Wanstead Music Centre   pianos
2 a) 130
  b) 75 pence
  c) 530 3808
3 For Christmas
4 Yes. The advert says, 'Get your <u>second</u> value-packed issue ...'
5 No. The advert says, 'Just ... pianos ...'
6 a) i) *Car Buyer* magazine
  b) i) Cuticura medicated soap
  c) iv) LBC Pop Review
  d) iii) Ariel automatic washing powder
  e) ii) Swift Interiors
7 a) 30 pence
  b) ... chemists everywhere
  c) 9.30 p.m.
  d) Quartz
  e) 205 2107

Answer key

UNIT 7 Terminal One

1 You should have underlined the following: Edinburgh, Cork, Ankara, Dublin, Cyprus (Larnaca), Canada, Athens, New York, Düsseldorf, Belfast
2 a) closing b) checking in c) boarding
3 Edinburgh; *Gate 4* Cork; *BA 838*; *Gate 9* Dublin; *AI 141*; *Closing* Athens; *BA 560*; *Gate 22*; *Closing*

4

Title	Forename	Surname	Travel information
Mr	Ian	Jackman	recently arrived from Ankara
Dr	Raymond	Miller	from Dublin
Ms	Yvonne	Simpson	from Cyprus
Mrs	———	Waring	meeting a passenger from Larnaca
Capt.	Jay	Brock	from Canada
Mr	Stephen	Sandberg	recently arrived from New York
Miss	Margaret	Murphy	in transit from Düsseldorf to Belfast

UNIT 8 The Touch of Death

1 c 2 d
3 a) 18
  b) Roberts
  c) Richmond 580311
4 c
5 c and e
6 a) True
  b) True
  c) False
  d) False
  e) True

UNIT 9 Dial-A-Recipe

1 1½ kg cooked, skinned chicken
   300 ml fresh mayonnaise
   150 ml soured cream
   1 tablespoonful paprika
   2 tablespoonfuls tomato puree
   ½ teaspoonful caster sugar
   4 large, chopped, skinned tomatoes
   a little salt
   freshly ground black pepper
2 Chris made four mistakes. They were
   (1) 1 kg chicken, instead of 1½ kg.
   (2) 300 ml soured cream, instead of 150 ml.
   (3) a teaspoonful paprika, instead of a tablespoonful.
   (4) ½ tablespoonful caster sugar, instead of ½ teaspoonful.
3 First, remove bones.
   Then, cut chicken into cubes.
   Next, mix all other ingredients (mayonnaise, cream, paprika, puree, sugar, tomatoes, salt and pepper).
   Then, add chicken.
   Now, stir (gently).
   Finally, chill for ½ hour, at least.
4 **Ingredients**
   ½ lettuce
   1 *bunch* watercress   (should be ½ *bunch*)
   ½ cucumber   (should be ¼ *cucumber*)
   ½ green pepper   (should be 1 *pepper*)
   1 spring onion   (should be *a few*)
   120 ml French *mustard* (should be French *dressing*)
   Method
   Core and seed the pepper. Chop or slice all the ingredients and mix with the French dressing.
   Variations
   For extra interest add *chopped*   (should be *thinly-sliced*)
   hard-boiled eggs, *lots of*   (should be *a little*)
   lemon juice, *a few*   (should be *lots of*)
   nuts, and some thin slices of *apple* (should be *avocado pear*)
   Add nuts only at the last minute.
5 Possible combinations:
   grated   apple, onion, cheese, cabbage
   chopped   grapefruit, apple, onion, cabbage, walnuts, celery, tomato
   minced   beef
   cored   apple
   skinned   chicken, cod, tomato
   boned   chicken, cod
   shelled   walnuts
   diced   grapefruit, chicken, apple, onion, beef, cabbage, walnuts, celery, tomato
   stoned   olives
   shredded   chicken, beef, cabbage
   peeled   grapefruit, apple, onion

UNIT 10 The Weather Forecast

1 It is probably early to mid-summer. The weather is described as warm and the night temperature will be no lower than 15 degrees in the south. There have been 15 hours of sunshine. It's probably Thursday, since we are told 'the outlook for Friday and the weekend'.
2 d
3
4 a) i)
  b) iii)
  c) ii)
  d) i)
5 a) x)   f) i)
  b) iii)   g) ii)
  c) ix)   h) iv)
  d) vii)   i) v)
  e) vi)   j) viii)

6 It was probably 8.58 p.m. (i.e. 20.58) because the weatherman first described what the weather had been like during the day.
7 a) two minutes past twelve
  b) seventeen minutes past four
  c) ten past nine
  d) quarter past one
  e) one minute to eleven

UNIT 11 Buying A New Car

1

	Model	Engine	Price	Petrol	Doors
MG Metro	1300	1300cc	£6299	56mpg	3
Volkswagen Golf	GL	1600cc	£8090	47mpg	5
Peugeot 205	XS	1400cc	£6225	54mpg	3
Renault 5	TSE	1400cc	£6675	56mpg	3
Ford Escort	GL	1400cc	£7182	57mpg	5

2 a) George
   b) £6,500
   c) It's too expensive for them and they think it's a little bit boring.
   d) Not really
   e) The Peugeot 205 XS

3 They probably chose the Peugeot 205 XS because
   i) it seemed to be George's favourite (even though he said he didn't like French cars)
   ii) Monica doesn't object to it
   iii) it is the cheapest and seems to be good value for money

4 a) windscreen wiper b) bonnet c) headlamp
   d) front bumper e) radiator grille f) aerial
   g) rear light h) rear bumper i) mud flap
   j) wing mirror

5 George seems to be a little more enthusiastic than Monica. Monica seems to be more concerned about how much they can afford and getting value for money. George seems more impressed by the appearance of the cars.

6

1 Scratches and badly finished paintwork
2 Not enough leg-room
3 Sunroof difficult to open
4 Wing mirror difficult to adjust
5 A lot of engine noise
6 Badly fixed plastic strip

7 a) iv) b) v) c) ii) d) i) e) iii)

UNIT 12 The London Marathon

1 b

2

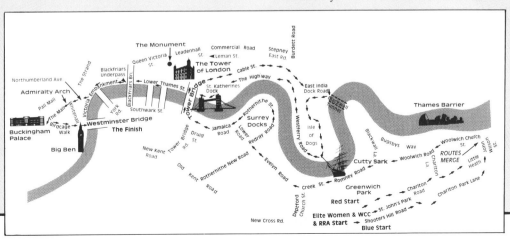

3

PREVIOUS WINNERS OF THE LONDON MARATHON				
YEAR	MEN	COUNTRY	WOMEN	COUNTRY
1981	Inge Simonsen Dick Beardsley	Norway USA	Joyce Smith	UK
1982	Hugh Jones	UK	Joyce Smith	UK
1983	Mike Gratton	UK	Greta Waitz	Norway
1984	Charlie Spedding	UK	Ingrid Kristiansen	Norway
1985	Steve Jones	UK	Ingrid Kristiansen	Norway

4 a) iii) b) iii) c) iv) d) ii) e) i)

UNIT 13 The People's Republic of China: Facts and Figures

1 a
2 Over four thousand years
3 The Soviet Union and Canada
4 One billion
5 2. USSR 3. Mongolia 6. India 10. Burma 11. Laos 12. Vietnam
6 c **7** d **8** 9,575,000 km^2 **9** 21%
10 A: Shanghai B: 9,500,000
    C: 8,000,000 D: 6,600,000
11 a) ii) d) iii)
    b) v) e) i)
    c) iv)
12 a) twenty-eight thousand and seventy-two kilometres
    b) six thousand two hundred and fifty square kilometres
    c) twenty-one per cent
    d) one third (*or* a third)
    e) one quarter (*or* a quarter)

UNIT 14 A Valuable Collection?

1 b **2** b **3** d **4** d **5** d
6 First reason: c
    Second reason: a
    Third reason: d
7 Probably not. He says he doesn't think he'd get very much money for it if he tried to sell it.

Answer key

UNIT 15 What's in a Name?

1 a, c, d, f, g
2 d   3 c   4 b   5 c   6 d   7 c   8 a
9 a) His Highness
   b) ... much the same as ...
   c) make
   d) ... call to mind ...
   e) ... evident disfavour ...
   f) ... refer to the matter ...

UNIT 16 'Value For Money'

1 Five
2 £26.95
3 12 months
4 a) KAFFEMATIC 25
   Made in West Germany
   Number of cups   12
   Free plug   YES
   Free coffee   YES
   Free filter papers   YES
   12 months guarantee
   Spare parts not mentioned
   Price   £29.95

   b) COFFEE MASTER De-luxe
   Made in the U.K.
   Number of cups   8
   Free plug   NO
   Free coffee   NO
   Free filter papers   YES
   12 months guarantee
   Spare parts not mentioned
   Price   £25.75

   c) DOMESTIKA ELECTRIC COFFEE POT
   Made in Czechoslovakia
   Number of cups   8
   Free plug   NO
   Free coffee   NO
   Free filter papers   NO
   12 months guarantee
   Spare parts will be difficult to find
   Price   £19.95

   d) AROMACUP 2000
   Made in Britain
   Number of cups   10
   Free plug   NO
   Free coffee   YES but only ½ kg
   Free filter papers   YES
   12 months guarantee
   Spare parts not mentioned
   Price   £22.50

   e) KAFFITALIA Automatic
   Made in Italy
   Number of cups   9
   Free plug   NO
   Free coffee   NO
   Free filter papers   YES
   12 months guarantee
   Spare parts not mentioned
   Price   £26.95

UNIT 17 Programming the Video

1 b
2 i) Is the machine switched on?
   ii) Is there a tape in it?
3 First RECORD and then PLAY
4 a) 8 b) 7 c) 2 d) 4 e) 6 f) 3 g) 5 h) 1
5 2–PROGRAMME 3–SET 4–STORE
6 Four
7 a) Channel selected: 4 Day: *Wednesday*
      Start time: *8.00* Finished time: *9.00*
   b) RESET

UNIT 18 The Department Store

1 BASEMENT Gardening
   GROUND FLOOR Customer Services, Food Halls
   FIRST FLOOR Sports
   SECOND FLOOR 'Ritz' Boutique
   THIRD FLOOR Coffee Shop
   FOURTH FLOOR Restaurant
2 a) £2.50   d) £9.95
   b) £12.99   e) £16.00
   c) £14.00   f) £9.50 to £95.00
3 a) True   e) False
   b) Probably false   f) Probably true
   c) Probably false   g) False
   d) Probably false   h) Probably true
      (the Restaurant   i) Probably true
      is air-conditioned)   j) True, if you spend £15 or more
4 a) SECOND
   b) GROUND
   c) BASEMENT
   d) SECOND
   e) SECOND

UNIT 19 Radio Phone-In

1 d
2 a) 15
   b) Manchester
   c) Christine
3 c
4 a) 28
   b) A shampoo
   c) No
5 3 years   6 No   7 d

UNIT 20 First Aid

1 b
2 d
3 c
4 c
5 1 soon as possible 2 cotton wool 3 press down
   4 5 minutes 5 wide open 6 hold 7 closed
   8 dressing 9 clean 10 doctor 11 piece of wood
   12 bleed 13 calm 14 drink 15 wet 16 water
6 a) ii)   d) iii)
   b) i)   e) ii)
   c) iii)